ANDALUSIA

Costa del Sol, Ronda, la Gibraltar, Tangier

Martin Gostelow

Mountain village CASARES

J·P·M

CONTENTS

This Way Andalusia

A Moorish Paradise

Think of Spain and the chances are that you think of Andalusia. This is the land of flamenco and bullfights, of dashing men on horseback, of dark eyes and dark secrets. Tiny white villages cling to the hillsides, medieval castles crown the summits, dazzling sunlight beats down on a bleached landscape. The historic cities of Granada, Córdoba and above all Seville can seem like stage sets, the air heavy with dramatic tension.

The region, called Andalucía in Spanish, took its name from the Vandals, though theirs was the briefest of rules, from 409 to 429, before they moved on to North Africa. To the Moors who came in the opposite direction and stayed for centuries, it was Al-Andalus, the closest they could imagine to an earthly paradise. More than 500 years have passed since their last strongholds fell to the Christian Reconquest, but the language and the landscape still carry the mark of the Moorish era, in its day the most advanced civilization of medieval Europe. Two of their creations, the Great Mosque of Córdoba and the Alhambra at Granada, rank among the world's greatest buildings.

Two Seas

Two contrasting coastlines face the Mediterranean and the Atlantic ocean. Inland are mountain ranges: the Sierra Nevada where snow lingers on the peaks well into summer, and the Serranía de Ronda encircling the eagle's nest city of Ronda. Orange and lemon orchards, vineyards and olive groves dress the gentler slopes and sheltered valleys; the rich plain of the Guadalquivir (from Wadi el-Kebir, Arabic for "great river") grows cotton and wheat.

Holidaymakers in their millions look no further than their chosen resort on the Costa del Sol, the cosmopolitan playground facing the Mediterranean. Guaranteed sunshine, a warm sea and low cost charter flights brought mass tourism to this coast in the 1960s, and changed it for ever. Little fishing villages all but disappeared behind a wall of hotels and apartments, and nearly everyone went to work for the holiday industry. But traditional life continues: fishing fleets put to sea before the tourists are awake, and each town has its weekly market. Málaga and Almería are still real working cities and ports.

The biggest resorts grew up next to the long, narrow beaches west of Málaga. Elsewhere the thin coastal strip is hemmed in by mountains which reach the sea in places to form cliffs and small coves. Inland, a different world is within easy reach: picturesque, sun-baked little towns of white-washed, red-tiled houses like a cubist painter's vision against a backdrop of majestic mountain scenery.

Atlantic Andalusia

The shorter Atlantic coast is surprisingly different. Tides wash broad expanses of golden sand, steady breezes send windsurfers flying over the waves. The tourism authorities promote it as the Costa de la Luz (Coast of Light), but there is rarely a crowd—visitor numbers are not even one-twentieth of those on the Costa del Sol. Those who do come are mostly Spanish, drawn to the beaches around the Bay of Cádiz and to the south near Cape Trafalgar, where old fishing ports are bursting their seams with new holiday villas and apartments.

Cádiz itself is a strange and ancient city, neglected but mesmeric, and unaccountably left out of most foreign visitors' travel plans.

Inland, cattle and horses graze the rolling pastures, bright green with early spring growth, baked yellow by the heat of summer. In Jerez de la Frontera, grapes grown on stony white slopes are turned into one of the world's classic wines, sherry.

Until the end of the 1970s, tourism was the only lively sector of the Andalusian economy. Otherwise the south was neglected by central government and left to ponder its past glories and plough on with its primitive agriculture. All that changed when democracy was restored. Spanish membership of the EU brought its largesse to poor regions, and the Expo-92 universal exposition stimulated the completion of new highways and high-speed rail links. Now with a large measure of autonomy, Andalusia has been booming.

1 THE MOST MAGNIFICENT MOSQUE In the 10th century **Córdoba** was the capital of Moorish Spain and the most cultured city in Europe. In its vast mosque, striped double arches are supported by over 800 classical columns set in rows that seem to stretch into an infinite distance. Even the Christian cathedral planted in the middle scarcely spoils the symmetry.

Flashback

Early Days

Before the seas reached their present level, Spain was joined to North Africa and the first inhabitants could walk from one continent to the other. Then, say the geologists, the Atlantic rose and began to pour in through the Straits of Gibraltar like a gigantic waterfall. Even so, it took centuries to fill the Mediterranean.

Around 30,000 BC, some of the last Neanderthals were living in caves in southern Spain. They died out, or were perhaps killed off by the first Cro-Magnon inhabitants, who left stone tools, bones and cave paintings, dating from 20,000 to 10,000 BC. Neolithic peoples made the short sea crossing from Africa in about 4000 BC, pioneered the cultivation of crops and built the massive stone burial chambers, or *dolmens*, which still stand today. Around the second millennium BC, a great civilization flourished near present-day Cádiz, the mysterious Tartessos, identified with the Biblical Tarshish. But it vanished with few traces, save some golden artefacts.

At about the same time Tartessos disappeared, Phoenicians from present-day Lebanon and Syria reached Spain by sea and set up trading posts along the coast. Naturally they chose the best anchorages—among them today's ports of Cádiz, Málaga and Almería.

Carthage and Rome

The Phoenician trading empire was taken over around 500 BC by their former colony, Carthage (in what is now Tunisia). The Carthaginians were drawn by Spain's mineral wealth, and pushed inland up the Guadalquivir valley, founding settlements at Seville and Córdoba.

When a dynamic new power, Rome, began to expand in the 3rd century BC, war was inevitable. The first round was indecisive, but in the second, Carthage used southern Spain as its base to attack Rome. Hannibal led his famous army across the Alps into Italy in 218 BC and scored signal victories, but then Rome invaded Spain and his supplies were cut off. In the end, Carthage was crushed and its possessions were added to the Roman Empire

The Romans stayed for 600 years, although it took the first two centuries to conquer the whole Iberian peninsula. Julius Caesar was a provincial governor for a time, and later put the city of 5

Córdoba to the sword when it backed his rival Pompey. Rome left towns, theatres, aqueducts and roads which can still be traced, but its greatest legacy was the Latin language, the forerunner of today's Spanish.

As imperial power declined, nomadic groups of barbarians from the north—Franks, Suevi, Alans—began to storm through Spain. At the start of the 5th century AD came the worst yet, the Vandals, whose name still stands for vicious destructiveness. Setting a thief to catch a thief, the Romans called on a marginally more civilized tribe of marauders, the Visigoths, for help. Adopting Roman ways, speaking Latin and converting to Christianity, they restored order and established a feudal state.

The Moors

After the death of the Prophet Mohammed in Arabia in AD 632, the new faith of Islam spread at lightning speed. By 683, Arab armies had conquered all of North Africa, where their converts included the warlike Berbers, or as they came to be known, the Moors. (The word was derived from Mauretania, the Roman name for what is now Morocco.)

Church tower in Marbella's old quarter adds an Andalusian touch.

Their eyes naturally turned to the rich lands of southern Spain, close enough to be seen across the narrow straits.

Invasion would have come sooner or later, but it was triggered by a dynastic squabble among Spain's Visigoth rulers, when one faction appealed to the Islamic leaders for help. In 711, a mainly Moorish army under the Arab general Tarik ibn-Ziyad landed near the promontory known afterwards as the Rock of Tarik (Jebel al-Tarik, or Gibraltar). Within seven years almost all of the Iberian peninsula was in their hands.

The huge Islamic empire, stretching from Baghdad to the Pyrenees, soon split up, the Spanish part becoming an independent Caliphate with its capital at Córdoba. Its tolerant rulers welcomed scholars of all faiths, and the city became one of Europe's greatest centres of culture.

In the 11th century the Caliphate in its turn fell apart into a patchwork of petty kingdoms, which gave Christian forces the chance to play one off against the other. New waves of Muslim zealots, the Almoravids and then the Almohads, crossed from North Africa to hold the line. They accused the Moors of living a life of luxury in Andalusia—before succumbing to its pleasures themselves.

7

Reconquest

Even at the high tide of Islam, Christian princes had retained a foothold in northern Spain. As early as the 10th century, they began to form the alliances that gradually pushed back the frontiers of Moorish rule.

La Reconquista (Reconquest) gathered pace in the 12th century with the capture of central Spain. Córdoba fell to the forces of Fernando III of Castile in 1236, followed by Seville in 1248. Meanwhile Castile's ally, and rival, Aragón had conquered the Mediterranean coast as far south as Alicante.

By the end of the 13th century, the Moors were confined to the mountains around Granada and Ronda, and the coasts of Málaga and Almería. And there the frontier stabilized for almost 200 years. The Christian kings had the upper hand, but preferred collecting tribute in gold from the Moors to fighting them. In the meantime, refugees from Seville and Córdoba had flocked to Granada, where the Nasrid kings presided over a last flowering of Moorish culture in Europe.

With the marriage in 1469 of Ferdinand (Fernando) and Isabella (Isabel), respective heirs to the kingdoms of Aragón and Castile, the stage was set for the last act of the Reconquest. They duly ascended their thrones as *Los Reyes Católicos*, the Catholic Monarchs, at the head of a united Spain, and their army marched on the last Moorish strongholds. Ronda fell in 1485, followed by Málaga and Almería. The king and queen themselves joined the siege of Granada, which surrendered on 2 January 1492.

World Power

In the year Granada fell, Columbus landed in the West Indies. For the next century and a half, explorers and adventurers, traders and priests headed for the New World, conquering vast territories and sending back gold, silver and gemstones in quantities previously undreamed of. It was Spain's Golden Age, but it could not last. Pirates preyed on Spanish coasts, ships and colonies, and her wealth was wasted in wars with European rivals. The marriage of Juana "La Loca" (the Mad), daughter of Ferdinand and Isabella, to Philip of Burgundy, had put the Habsburgs on the Spanish throne, and they were often more concerned with their lands and ambitions in northern Europe. Then the Reformation split the Christian world and intolerance reigned. Moors and Jews had been given the "choice" of expulsion or conversion, but now even the converts were suspect, and suffered persecution, death, or exile.

Troubled Times

In 1700, the half-witted Carlos II died without an obvious heir. France put forward a Bourbon claimant; Britain backed an Austrian Habsburg. In the War of the Spanish Succession (1702–13), British forces seized Gibraltar, and held on to it under the Treaty of Utrecht which ended the war and awarded the Bourbons the throne.

In 1805, Spanish ships fought alongside the French against Nelson's British fleet at Trafalgar; the survivors limped into Cádiz. Napoleon came to suspect his ally of seeking a separate peace; in 1808 he sent in French troops and replaced King Ferdinand VII with his own brother, Joseph Bonaparte. Spain rose in revolt and with the help of the British army commanded by the Duke of Wellington, the French were eventually driven out. The campaign, called the Peninsular War in Britain, is known to the Spanish as the War of Independence. Spain's first constitution was drawn up by the Cortes (Parliament) in Cádiz in 1812, although it did not survive the return of King Ferdinand.

While Spain was in turmoil, most of its possessions in the New World seized the chance to declare their independence. The rest of the 19th century was punctuated by wars over the succession, short term republican regimes and military coups. Colonial war in Morocco brought defeat in 1921, and in 1923 General Primo de Rivera became dictator; King Alfonso XIII remained on the throne, but as a spectator. Primo de Rivera was ousted in 1929, and when elections in 1931 showed the extent of republican sentiment, both he and the Spanish king went into exile.

PIRATES

For many centuries, until less than 200 years ago, the coasts of southern Europe were almost depopulated. Few dared live close to the sea, unless within the walls of a strongly fortified port. Picturesque fishing villages are a relatively modern creation. In those days watchtowers crowned cliffs and hilltops; lookouts anxiously scanned the horizon for hostile ships and signalled warnings to flee inland. Most feared were the Barbary corsairs from North Africa who came in search of plunder and slaves. Fit men who were caught faced a life chained to the oars in the pirates' galleys. Except for the rich who could be ransomed, their only hope of release was defeat in battle with a Christian fleet—but then they were more likely to drown.

Antequera sits in a fertile valley presided over by the Peña de los Enamorados (Lovers' Rock), considered to resemble a man's profile.

Civil War and After

The republic proclaimed in April 1931 soon faced attempted army rebellions. Its supporters responded with strikes and church-burnings, and a vicious circle of assassinations led to the murder of the rightwing opposition leader Calvo Sotelo in 1936. Five days later, on 17 July, the military garrison of Melilla rose in revolt, and army units in Seville, Cádiz and many other cities quickly followed suit. Led by General Francisco Franco, these Nationalist forces were generally supported by monarchists, the Church and rightwing parties. Opposing them was the Republican government, backed by liberals, socialists, the trade unions, communists and anarchists. To augment the small part of the armed forces which remained loyal, it created a popular army from local militia and untrained civilians.

The Civil War which ensued was fought with unremitting savagery. In city or village, the side in control would round up its opponents—or mere suspects—to be shot or, as at Ronda, hurled over a precipice. When a place changed hands, reprisals were merciless.

Both sides received aid from abroad. Fascist Italy and Nazi Germany sent troops, ships and air squadrons to help the Nationalists. The Soviet Union provided weapons, aircraft and pilots to the Republican government, and tens of thousands of volunteers from many countries fought for the Republican cause in the International Brigades. After almost three years of facing the superior firepower and training of the Nationalists and their more effective allies, the government forces collapsed.

Franco was able to keep Spain out of World War II and the exhausted nation began to recover. In the 1950s, the fashion for holidays in the sun brought increasing numbers of foreign visitors. Fishing villages on the Costa del Sol were transformed by a rash of hotel-building as jet travel and package deals multiplied the tourist count into millions.

New Horizons

In 1969, Franco named a successor, the young grandson of Alfonso XIII, who was proclaimed King Juan Carlos I after the old dictator died in 1975. Rightwing forces expected him to continue in Franco's footsteps, but he was determined to assure rapid progress to democracy. Showing a genius for reconciliation, he managed the transition brilliantly, and then stood back to become the kind of constitutional monarch the country had never known. Even die-hard republicans were compelled to admiration.

Spain joined NATO in 1981 and the European Union in 1986, a profound change from the days of Franco when she was an outcast from the rest of Europe. Completing the transformation, Franco's repression of regional aspirations was replaced by toleration, and European funds began to make an impact on rural poverty. Faced with competition from Greece, Turkey and other holiday magnets, the Costa del Sol started to clean up its beaches and streets, clamp down on petty crime and pay more attention to the environment that had attracted the visitors in the first place.

2 THE TWO MOST BEAUTIFUL PALACES The **Alhambra** at Granada is an Arabian Nights dream, the ultimate expression of Moorish artistry. Marble pavilions and courtyards are covered with arabesque designs of astonishing detail and delicacy. Moors under Christian rule built the **Alcázar** of Seville, smaller than the Alhambra but exquisitely decorated.

Cabeza del Buey

Castuera

Almendralejo

Sta. Marta

Almendral

Villafranca de los Barros

Belalcázar

Zafra

Los Santos

Valencia de las Torres

Villanueva del Duque

Jerez de los Caballeros

Liérana

Peñarroya-Pueblonuevo

Pozobla

Fregenal de la Sierra

N 630

Azuaga

CÓRDOBA

Monesterio

Villaviciosa de Córdoba

N 432

PORTUGAL

Galaroza

Alanís

Embalse de Bembézar

Rosal de la Frontera

Aracena

Sta. Olalla del Cala

Cazalla

Córdoba

Sta. Barbara

Jabugo

Río Tinto

N 433

Constantina

Posadas

Cabezas Rubias

Minas de Río Tinto

El Ronquillo

El Pedroso

Río Guadalquivir

Calañas

N 435

Los Pajanosas

Castilblanco de los Arroyos

Lora del Rio

Écija

HUELVA

Valverde del Camino

Las

Pue Ger

Río Guadiana

Gibraleón

La Palma del Condado

Niebla

Sanlúcar la Mayor

N 630

Carmona

A 4

SEVILLA

S. Bartolomé de la Torre

Moguer

N 442

Sevilla

Marchena

N 431

Huelva

Palos de la Frontera

El Rocio

Los Palacios y Villafranca

Utrera

El Arahal

Osuna

A 92

Torre de la Higuera

Parque Nacional de Doñana

Las Marismas

N IV

N 333

Las Cabezas de San Juan

Morón de la Frontera

Campille

Golfo de Cádiz

N 339

Villamartin

Algodonales

N 342

Teba

El Cuervo

Bornos

Cuevas de Becerr

Sanlúcar de Barrameda

El Bosque

Grazalema

Torrecilla 1919 m

Jeréz de la Frontera

Arcos de la Frontera

Ronda

Rota

A 4

CÁDIZ

Ubrique

Sierra de Rond

El Puerto de Sta. María

Cádiz

San Fernando

Medina-Sidonia

Jimena de la Frontera

N 339

Marb

Chiclana de la Frontera

Vejer de la Frontera

N 440

A 340

Estepona

Cabo de Trafalgar

Sotogrande

Bahía de Marbella

ATLANTIC

Barbate

Los Barros

Gibraltar

OCEAN

Costa de la Luz

N 340

Algeciras

Tarifa

Tanger

Ceuta

MOROCCO

Valdepeñas

Puertollano

Villanueva
de los Infantes

Alcaraz

Brazatortas

Almuradiel

Elche de
la Sierra

A 4

La Carolina

JAÉN

N 322

Orcera

Cardeña

Baños de
la Encina

Villacarrillo

Pontones

El Moral

Montoro

Andújar

Linares

Úbeda

Puebla de
Don Fadrique

Mengíbar

Peal de
Becerro

Porcuna

Martos

Jódar

Cazorla

Huéscar

ampiña

Jaén

N 321

Sierra de
la Pandera
1845 m

Mancha
Real

Pozo
Alcón

GRANADA

Vélez
Rubio

astro del Rio

ntilla

Baena

Campillo
de Arenas

Guadahortuna

Baza

Cúllar Baza

uilar

Cabra

Alcalá
la Real

A 92

Caniles

Huércal-
Overa

Lucena

Priego
de Córdoba

N 323

Darro

Santa Bárbara
2269 m

N 323

Olula
del Rio

Tejar

N 331

N 432

Pinos
Puente

Diezma

Guadix

Sierra de Baza

Tetica
2080 m

Sierra de los Filabres

Moraleda
de Zafayona

A 92

Granada

Mulhacen
3482 m

N 324

Abla

Sierra Nevada

ALMERÍA

idona

Salinas

Ventas
de Huelma

Pico Veleta
3398 m

Tabernas

A 340

ntequera

Periana

Alhama
de Granada

Padul

Lanjarón

Níjar

rcal

ÁLAGA

Béznar

Orgiva

Cádiar

Láujar de
Andarax

Almería

N 331

Vélez-
Málaga

Sierra

Almijara

Motril

Berja

Cabo
de Gata

Málaga

Torre
del Mar

Nerja

Almuñecar

Calahonda

El Ejido

Golfo
de Almería

Torremolinos

Bahía de Málaga

engirola

C o s t a   d e l   S o l

MEDITERRANEAN

SEA

0   40 km

N

ANDALUSIA

Map of Sevilla

Palacio de las Dueñas

San Andrés

Pl. de la Encarnación

Sta. Catalina

Pl. Ponce de León

E. Pías

Museo de las Bellas Artes

Pl. del Museo

Alfonso XII

Concordia

Teniente Borges

Martín Villa

Laraña

Antigua Universidad

Imagen

San Pedro

Pl. Doña Carmen

Pl. Cristo de Burgos

Convento San Leandro

Casa de Pilatos

Magdalena

Palacio Lebrija

Don Alonso el Sabio

San Ildefonso

Alcaicería

San Pablo

Pl. de Godines

Pl. Salvador

S. Salvador

Huelva

Pescadería

Aguilas

Reyes Católicos

Zaragoza

San Isidoro

Corral del Rey

San Nicolás

Pl. Nueva

Ayunta-miento

BARRIO

Santa María la Blanca

Mercado de Entradores

Adriano

Palacio Arzo-bispal

Guzmán el Bueno

DE

Pl. Curtidores

La Maestranza

Catedral

Pl. de los Reyes

SANTA CRUZ

Santa Cruz

La Giralda Casa Lonja

Pl. del Triunfo

Hospital Venerables

Pl. S.Cruz

Pl. Refina-dores

Teatro de la Maestranza

Maestranza Artillería

Archivo de Indias

Pl. Doña Elvira

Santa Ana

Alcázar

Monumento a Colón

Torre del Oro

Puerta de Jerez

Jardines de los R. R. Alcázares

Jardines de Murillo

Pl. de Cuba

Jardines de Cristina

San Fernando

Av. de Cádiz

Avenida de Malaga

Palacio S. Telmo

Universidad

Pl. Don Juan de Austria

Avenida de Carlos

Jardines de San Telmo

Teatro L. de Vega

Gta. San Diego

Avenida de Portugal

Río Guadalquivir

Parque de

Plaza de España

Gta. de los Marineros Voluntarios

Pte. del Generalisimo

María Luisa

N

300 m

300 yd

SEVILL

On the Scene

Andalusia is compact enough to let you see most of the highlights in a couple of weeks, yet as full of variety as you could wish, starting with the three beautiful inland cities of the south: Seville, Córdoba and Granada. Celebrated in song and legend, their monuments from the Moorish era are world-renowned. Then comes the holiday playground of the Costa del Sol, moving from east to west. The last section of this guide covers the Atlantic coast, the Costa de la Luz, the ancient port of Cádiz and Jerez de la Frontera, home of sherry.

GOLDEN TRIO
Seville, Córdoba, Granada

You can visit the historic inland cities one at a time on excursions from your seaside base, although you'll spend a lot of time on the road or in the train, and have to do your sightseeing in the heat of the day. A better plan would be to stay in each city; Granada demands a couple of days, Córdoba an overnight stop, and Seville at least three.

Seville *(Sevilla)*
In Spain's Golden Age, when galleons carried the treasures of the New World up the Guadalquivir River, people said: "Madrid may be the capital of Spain, but Seville is the capital of the world". When the crowds gather for the Easter Holy Week ceremonies or for the parades, bullfights and fireworks of the April Fair *(La Feria de Abril)*, it can still feel like the only place to be. The capital of Andalusia, Seville is an industrial and commercial hub, with a population of 700,000, but most visitors are more concerned with its romantic past: the Moorish-style fortress, the magnificent cathedral, the palaces, fountains and gardens.

The city began as an Iberian settlement near the mouth of the Guadalquivir. Romans, Carthaginians, Vandals and Visigoths followed, and then five centuries of Moorish rule when the city became a great centre of culture.

After the Christian Reconquest, it was the base for voyages of exploration and the designated port of entry for ships bringing back the wealth of the Americas.

Hard times came when the city was hit by plague, the river silted up, the monopoly on American trade was revoked and, in the 19th century, the Latin American colonies were lost. In the Civil War, Seville quickly fell to Franco's Nationalists. His regime suppressed regional aspirations, but with the restoration of democracy Andalusia became an autonomous region, with Seville as its capital. The city celebrated the 500th anniversary of the voyage of Columbus by inviting the world to Expo 92. Dredging of the river enables cargo and cruise ships of up to 15,000 tonnes to reach Seville, though it is 100 km (62 miles) from the sea.

The famous buildings are concentrated within walking distance in the historic centre, on the east bank of the Guadalquivir. Horse-drawn carriages wait in the Plaza de Triunfo near the Cathedral to take you on a city tour. (Find out the cost before embarking.) Open-top buses offer another way to see the sights restfully; their main pickup point is opposite the riverside Torre del Oro.

The Cathedral

For a long time after the Reconquest, the Christians worshipped in the former great mosque, reconsecrated as their cathedral. Then in 1401 they resolved to replace it with what is still the biggest Gothic church ever built. ("Let us build a church so large the world will think us mad," the city fathers are said to have proclaimed.) Construction took over a century.

The fortress-like exterior is relieved by decorative pinnacles and extravagantly carved stone doorways. Inside, 40 columns soar into the brilliantly lit vault of the immense nave. The main chapel and choir stand like two central islands, the choir with an elaborate iron grille and beauti-

THE THREE GREATEST CATHEDRALS In **Seville** they built the biggest Gothic church in the world, and one of the most dramatic. **Málaga** cathedral has an unfinished tower, but it is full of treasures and takes the trouble to explain them. The "new" 18th-century **Cádiz** cathedral stands by the sea, like a white stone fortress glistening in the sun.

fully carved choir stalls in arabesque designs. Double aisles are lined by many side chapels filled with art treasures, including pictures by Murillo, Zurbarán, Goya and della Robbia.

The Royal Chapel (*Capilla Real*) contains the tomb of Ferdinand III of Castile, who took Seville from the Moors in 1248, and the bones of Christopher Columbus are presumed to lie in a 19th century monument in the form of a coffin carried by four powerful figures, in the south transept. It was brought back from Havana (the monument as well as the remains) after the loss of Cuba in 1898. A cross in the treasury is said to have been made from the small amount of gold the explorer brought back from his first voyage to the New World.

The oval Chapterhouse in the southeast corner is a marvel of restraint in so grandiose a building, with a number of wall-paintings by Murillo.

The Giralda

The tower adjoining the cathedral, 95 m (312 ft) high, was originally built as the minaret of the Great Mosque and later converted into a bell tower. Up to the mid-section it is built of patterned brick and dates from the 12th century; the elaborate upper part was added in the 16th century. It was crowned by the figure of Faith which served as a weathervane *(giraldillo)* and gave the tower its name, but after four centuries of wear and tear the bronze image has been removed, with plans to replace it with a replica. The climb to the top is by a 340-m (375-yd) interior brick ramp, easier than if there were steps and well worth the effort; the views are magnificent. (The ramp allowed Ferdinand III to ride to the top on his horse and survey his new conquest.)

Also surviving from the Moorish era is the Court of the Orange Trees *(Patio de los Naranjos)*, below the Giralda and adjoining the north wall of the cathedral. It was the main courtyard of the mosque, cool and shaded and with fountains for the ritual washing which was required before entering. Still planted with orange trees, it serves as a dusty transit area for visitors.

Casa Lonja

Facing the Plaza de Triunfo between the Cathedral and the Alcázar is the former exchange building, the Casa Lonja, designed in the 16th century by Juan de Herrera, architect of the huge, austere Escorial Palace near Madrid. Nowadays it contains the Archives of the Indies *(Archivo de Indias)*, a priceless collection of 36,000 documents on the dis- 17 covery of the Americas, including letters written by Columbus and Magellan.

Alcázar

Built on the site of the Moorish citadel, Al Kasr in Arabic, a royal palace was begun in the reign of Pedro the Cruel of Castile in the 14th century. Little of the earlier building was preserved, but the replacement has typically Moorish arches and intricate decorative details, the work of Mudéjar artisans and designers.

The Court of the Maidens (*Patio de las Doncellas*), surrounded by a graceful marble colonnade, leads to the imposing Hall of the Ambassadors (*Salón de los Embajadores*), where the walls are covered with intricate Arabic script, including quotations from the Koran. On the floor above are the former royal apartments used by Ferdinand of Aragón and Isabella of Castile, whose marriage united Spain under one crown. Enormous 18th-century Madrid tapestries, superb copies of Flemish originals, hang in the rooms created for Emperor Charles V. Down in the basement, vaulted Arab baths survived from the Moorish era. They were adapted to other uses after the Reconquest, as the Christians were not yet aware that there may be a link between cleanliness and godliness.

The Alcázar's great complex of walled gardens spreads to the south and east of the palace. Orange, cypress and palm trees shade the paths; fountains play among the rose beds while ducks and golden carp share the pools.

Barrio de Santa Cruz

East of the palace and the cathedral is a maze of alleys, so narrow in places that upper storey balconies almost touch. Once the Jewish quarter, it became the home of the nobility in the 17th century and there are still many gracious white-painted houses with flower-decked patios hidden behind high walls. Nearer the cathedral it has been taken over by souvenir shops, *tapas* bars and restaurants, bookshops and antique dealers. The painter Murillo lived at Santa Teresa No 8.

The House of Pilate (*Casa de Pilatos*) to the northeast was built in the 16th century as a supposed copy of Pontius Pilate's house in Jerusalem. It has superb stucco work, tiles and elegant arcaded courtyards.

South of the Centre

The massive, rather dour 18th-century building next to the south wall of the Alcázar Gardens, now

The Giralda Tower was originally the minaret of the Grand Mosque.

the University, was once the tobacco factory *(Fábrica de Tabacos)* where thousands of women worked, rolling cigars. Famously fractious, immodest and impertinent, these *cigarreras* were the model for the fictional Carmen.

To the south is Parque María Luisa, created for a 1929 Iberian-American Exhibition. Some of the buildings were permanent, notably around the semi-circular Plaza de España and the baroque-revival Archaeological Museum *(Museo Arqueológico)* at the southern end of the park, facing Plaza de América.

Along the River

The riverside promenade was given a facelift for the 1992 Exposition and 500th anniversary of the voyage of Columbus to the New World. You can stroll or sit at an open-air café, watch rowing crews practising or racing, or take a cruise up and down the Guadalquivir on an excursion boat.

The 13th-century Golden Tower *(Torre del Oro)* is a remnant of Seville's Moorish fortifications. The name recalls the colour of the tiles that once covered its walls. Inside is a small maritime museum.

Across the riverside avenue, Paseo de Cristóbal Colón, stands one of the world's newest opera houses, the Teatro de la Maestranza. It opened in time for

Expo-92 with, naturally, a performance of *Carmen*.

Further along the river bank, to the west of the cathedral, the neo-classical Maestranza bullring *(Plaza de Toros)* is one of the largest in Spain, seating 14,000, and also one of the oldest. Pedro Romero from Ronda, "father of the bullfight", appeared here in the 18th century.

Museo de las Bellas Artes

North and away from the river, the Fine Arts Museum is housed in an old convent, La Merced, its wonderful church serving as the main gallery. The emphasis is on the school of Seville and its leading exponents, Pacheco, Zurbarán and Murillo, with a portrait by El Greco of his son and an early work by Velázquez.

Triana

Across the river on the west (right) bank, the sprawling Triana district is an area of factories, small shops and modest housing. It was once known as the gypsy quarter and retains a tradition of *flamenco*, sometimes seen in the bars and clubs.

Isla de la Cartuja

A swampy island in the Guadalquivir, 3 km (2 miles) north of the city centre was transformed when it was chosen as the site of Expo-92. Most of the pavilions were only temporary, but the rest have been turned into business premises, a science research facility and a theme park, Isla Mágica, with a fun fair, cinemas and other entertainments.

The only old building is the Cartuja itself, a former Carthusian monastery where Christopher Columbus was buried after his death in 1507. Eventually, his wish was respected and his remains were sent to the island of Hispaniola in the Caribbean. They were later moved to Havana in Cuba, and back to Seville in 1899 to lie in the cathedral (see p. 17), although some say that the bones returned were not his, but those of his son Diego. The monastery buildings were used as a ceramic factory until 1980; some of the kilns have been preserved and the church has been restored.

Itálica

About 10 km (6 miles) northwest of Seville lie the extensive ruins of the Roman city of Itálica, the birthplace of the 2nd-century emperors Hadrian and Trajan. Its amphitheatre was once one of the largest in existence, able to hold 40,000 spectators, more than the city's entire population. Some of the rows of seats and the underground passages still survive, and the street pattern and house foundations can be seen. Many mosaic floors were removed to Seville in past centuries but more have since been excavated. Some of the best finds can be admired in Seville's Archaeological Museum.

Córdoba

The capital of the Roman province of Hispania Ulterior, Córdoba rose to even greater glory under the Moors as one of the foremost cities of the medieval world. After the 8th-century Islamic conquest, it was the seat of governors who ruled most of Spain. In the 10th century, an independent caliphate of the western Muslim empire was declared, with Córdoba as its capital. The most eminent philosophers, scientists and physicians of the time gathered there. Christians and Jews were welcomed; it was the home of Maimonides, the great Jewish scholar and physician, and the philosopher Averroes. Caliph Al-Hakam II (961–976) assembled the biggest library of the day; and the most skilled artisans were engaged in building and beautifying palaces and mosques.

The caliphate broke up into petty kingdoms in the 11th century, enabling the resurgent Christians to play one against another. In 1236, Córdoba was captured by the forces of Ferdinand III of Castile. It is said that 21

CÓRDOBA

0 — 300 m
0 — 300 yd

Av. del Ollerías

Muro de la Misericordia

Carcamo

C. Marroquíes

Moriscos

Estación

Av. América

Doce de Octubre

Reyes Católicos

Pl. de Colón

Santa Marina

Alhaken II.

Av. del

Palacio de Viana

San Agus

Fr. L. de Granada

Ronda de los Tejares

Pl. Ruiz de Alda

Sta. Marina

Sta. Isabel

Ocaña

Is. Peral

Sta. María II

Av. de Cervantes

Gran Capitán

José Cruz Conde

C. del Osario

C. Conde Torres Cabrera

Pl. del Rincón

Alfaros

Ambrosio

Juan Rufo

Enrique Redel

López Diéguez

Realejo

San Hipólito

C. Góngora

Pl. San Miguel

Alfonso XIII.

San Pablo

San Andrés

Concepción

Paseo de la Victoria

C. Gondomar

Pl. de la Tendillas

Claudio Marcelo

Calvo Sotelo

Pal. de Orive

San Pablo

Ayuntamiento

Gutiérrez de los Ríos

Alcántara

C. Sevilla

Jesús y María

Pedro López

Pl. de la Corredera

Pl. San Pedro

López de Hoces

Casa de los Hoces

Sta. Victoria

C. Barrosa

Darío de Córdoba

Maese Luis

Mercado

Agu Mor

San Juan

Jerónimo Páez

Museo Arqueológico

San Francisco

Museo Julio Romero de Torres

Casa del Indiano

Arco

San Fernando

Museo de Bellas Artes

Puerta de Almódovar

Almanzor

Rey Heredia

Pl. Benavente

Caldereros

Posada del Potro

Paseo de la Ribe

BARRIO DE LA

Museo Taurino y Zoco

San Bartolomé

Cardenal Herrero

Pl. Abadez

Río Guadalquivir

Dr. Barroso

Av. Dr. Fleming

JUDERÍA

Mezquita-Catedral

Ronda de Isasa

Acera Mira al Río

Camposanto de los Mártires

Amador de los Ríos

Santo Cristo

Puente Romano

Alcázar de los Reyes Cristianos

Av. del Alcázar

Postrera

Pl. Rastro

Virrey Noja

Pl. Sta. Teresa

3,000 mosques and shrines were razed, but at least the Great Mosque was largely preserved.

The main sights are concentrated in the old city, just north of the Guadalquivir. The bridge over the river, still in use, stands on Roman foundations. Until the Middle Ages, it marked the furthest point that sea-going ships could reach. A restored waterwheel on the north bank is a reminder of Arab skills in supplying the baths and fountains of their cities. At the southern end of the bridge, a 14th-century tower houses a small museum of Córdoba's Moorish history.

La Mezquita

Begun in the 8th century, enlarged in the 9th and 10th, Córdoba's Great Mosque has been the model and inspiration for countless others throughout the Muslim world to this day. Under the caliphate it ranked with the Grand Mosque at Mecca and Al-Aksa in Jerusalem as one of the holiest places of Islam.

The building is rectangular, surrounded by buttressed walls. Most of the original doors are blocked, although some idea of their beauty can be gained from the surviving decoration on the east wall. The most dramatic entrance is by the northwest door, the Puerta del Perdón, opening onto the Patio de los Naranjos (Courtyard of the Orange Trees), shaded by orange and palm trees. A door in the opposite wall leads into a dark forest of more than 800 columns, supporting striped double horseshoe arches. The columns were brought here from ancient Roman and Byzantine sites all over Spain, North Africa and even from the eastern Mediterranean. Some are of marble, in many colours, some of other stone, a few of wood. In the far wall is the *mihrab*, the niche marking the direction of Mecca. Three domes above it are exquisitely carved; the central dome in particular is richly covered in tiles and mosaics of a lovely golden hue.

The victorious Christians in 1236 could not bring themselves to destroy anything so beautiful, but 16th-century church leaders were less sympathetic. They decreed that a cathedral should be planted right in the middle of the mosque. Emperor Charles V, who had been in favour of the project, was appalled when he saw the result. "You have built something that could have been built anywhere," he said, "but you have destroyed something unique." Even so, the Gothic and baroque intruder is undeniably striking, with its statues, gilding, moulded stucco, marble and magnificently carved mahogany choir stalls.

23

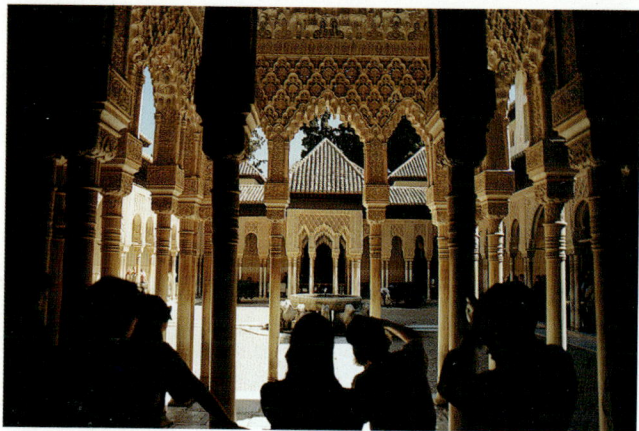

Forest of columns in Córdoba's Mosque, the crown jewel of Islamic Spain.

Alcázar

The buildings of the former royal palace date from the 14th century but they incorporate courtyards from the Moorish citadel and the lower levels include Moorish baths. From even earlier periods, Roman mosaics and stone sarcophagi are on display, and excavations continue. The terraced gardens which face down to the river are enlivened by fountains and streams.

Barrio de la Judería

The former Jewish quarter is an intriguing maze of winding streets and narrow alleys. Low whitewashed houses are half covered with flowers; arches lead to lush, typically Andalusian patios. In Calle de los Judios, a little synagogue was one of only three to survive after the expulsion of the Jews from Spain in 1492. Close by is a statue of the 12th-century philosopher Maimonides. Less commercial than Seville's Barrio de Santa Cruz, the Judería is known today for some of the city's best restaurants and *tapas* bars.

Museums

Córdoba's Fine Arts Museum *(Museo Provincial de Bellas Artes)* in Plaza de Potro has pictures by Spanish masters Murillo,

Zurbarán and Ribera as well as later artists. The Archaeological Museum housed in a fine old palace *(Palacio de Jerónimo Paéz)* has well-displayed collections of prehistoric, Roman, Moorish and medieval Christian treasures and artefacts.

Medina Azahara

On a terraced hillside some 8 km (5 miles) northwest of Córdoba stand the remains of one of the most beautiful palaces ever built. Construction began on the orders of Caliph Abd-el-Rahman III around the year 936, and according to Arab historians, 10,000 men laboured on the project for 25 years. Thousands of marble columns were brought from near and far; decoration was the ultimate in arabesque fantasy; the result was worthy of the capital of Al-Andalus. Again according to the chroniclers of the day, the palace-city was garrisoned by 12,000 soldiers, staffed by 4,000 servants and the stables held 2,000 horses.

Within 75 years, all this magnificence was gone, destroyed by Berber zealots who disapproved of such luxury. For centuries the site was looted for its marble and other building material, then it was forgotten. Scarcely one stone stood on another, so complete was the devastation. In recent years archaeologists have painstakingly separated the layers of debris, discovering complete sections of collapsed roof, lying on well-preserved floors. Buildings have been meticulously reconstructed and work continues to recreate as much as possible of this unique 10th-century Xanadu.

Granada

Islam made its last stand in Spain at Granada, over 250 years after the fall of Córdoba and Seville to the Christian Reconquest. This remnant of Moorish territory had survived so long through diplomacy and by paying tribute to the kings of Castile, but when Christian Spain was finally united under Ferdinand and Isabella, its days were numbered. After a siege lasting seven months, Granada surrendered on January 2, 1492, inaugurating a year in which Columbus was to sail the Atlantic and, less gloriously, Spain's Jews were to be offered the choice of exile or forced "conversion".

The defeated Moorish king, Boabdil, who handed over the keys of the city to the Catholic monarchs before heading for exile, wept when he looked back at what he had lost. His last view of Granada is for many visitors their first, from a pass on the road from Motril known as El Puerto del Suspiro del Moro (The Pass of the Moor's Sigh).

25

GRANADA

N

0 _____ 300 m
0 _____ 300 yd

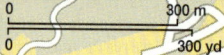

Pl. Cruz
de Piedra

Calle S. Luis

Cuesta de Chapiz

Río Darro

Generalife

Pl. Albaida

Internado
Ave María

Cuesta del Rey Chico

C. de Pagés

El Salvador

ALBAICIN

Pl.
Larga

Cta. A. de
Trillo

de
los
Reyes

Población

Alhambra

Museo Ca
Manuel de Fa

Carretera de Murcia

San Cristóbal

S. Nicolás

Zafra

Juan

Palacio
Carlos V

Antequeruela
Alta

Muralias
de Albaicín

Sta. María la Miel

Museo
Arqueológico
Provincial

Alcazaba

Paseo Central

Callejón Niño del Ro

Cuesta de la Alhacaba

Pilar Seco Gurniel

Santa Isabel
la Real

S.

Carrera del Darro

Baños
Arabes

C. de Santa Ana

Torre de
la Vela

REALEJO

Plegadero Alto

C. de la
Tiña

Camil Zenete

Pl. S.
Miguel
Bajo

C. de Sta. Ana

Santa Ana

Audiencia

P. de
Sta. Ana

Cuesta de Gomerez

Campo
Príncipe

Calle de Molin

Pl. del
Triunfo

Cta. de Marañas

Pl.
Nueva

Cuesta del Aire

Rodrigo
del Campo

Pl. del
Realejo

C. Santiago

Paco
Seco de Luce

Calle de Elvira

Pl. de Isabel
la Católica

Sta. Ecolástica

C. de San Matías

Capitanía

Pl. de los
Campos

Real
Sto. Doming

Gran Vía de Colón

Capilla
Real

Corral
de Carbón

Pl. Mariana Concepción
Pineda

C. de la
Concepción

C. S. Paula

C. de la Carce

Catedral

i

C. Reyes Católicos

Ayuntamiento

S. Jacin

C. de
Arriola

Santos Susto
y Pastor

San Jerónimo

Pl. de las
Pasiegas

Avg Gaviat

San Juan
de Dios

San Juan
de Dios

C. de

Pl. de
Bib-Rambla

Puerta
Real

Av. de Jose Antonio

Rector
Lóp. Árqueta

Universidad

C. de la Duquesa

Acera de Darro

Monasterio
S. Jerónimo

Pl. de los
Lobos

C. del Gran Capitán

Pl. de la
Trinidad

C. de las Tablas

C. de la Alhóndiga

C. P.árraga

Calle de San Antón

Pl. del
Gran Capitán

Camil del Picón

Callejón de Nevot

Calle de Puentezuelas

Verónica de la Magdalena

C. San Miguel Alta

Calle de la Cruz

C. del Angel

Calle de Recogidas

C. San José Baja

C. S. Miguel Bajo

C. Marqu.
de los
Vélez

Calle Telero

Calle de Alhamar

The city's setting is superb, with the Sierra Nevada as backdrop, and the heights of medieval Islamic architecture were reached in the Alhambra. A combination of palace, fortress, park and garden over a kilometre (1100 yd) long, it rises above the steep slopes of the valley of the River Darro. The old Moorish town of Albaicín across the river was a run-down area for centuries: now it has become quite fashionable and many houses have been restored. On the hillside north of the Alhambra, Sacromonte was the gypsy quarter for centuries and a few gypsy families still live there. Flamenco shows are staged in Sacromonte's caves, but they are a notorious tourist trap designed to separate visitors from their money.

Alhambra

When the Moors lost Seville and Córdoba, the most skilled artisans migrated to Granada, the last major city still in Muslim hands in Andalusia. They and their descendants created the Alhambra, a name derived from the Arabic for "the red", referring to the reddish-brown bricks of the outer walls.

It's a long walk up from the city, and with a lot more walking within the Alhambra complex, an ideal plan would be to stay overnight at one of the hotels near the entrance—or even inside the walls, in the State-run parador (though you'd have to reserve a few months in advance). It's well worth making the effort to enter at opening time, generally 9 a.m., avoiding the crowds which flood in towards the middle of the day. The ticket office is at the southeastern end—the most distant point from the city—and tickets are marked with a 30-minute time slot for entry to the Royal Palace (once you are inside, you can linger as long as you like). The allocated time may be up to two hours ahead at busy periods, but there is plenty to do in the interim. If you have more than an hour to spend, it would be worth visiting the Generalife gardens first, or the palace of Charles V and its museums. The Alcazaba needs about half an hour.

Furthest from the gate and nearest the river, the Alcazaba is a 9th-century castle, with a magnificent panorama from the top of its watchtower, the Torre de la Vela. But the heart of the Alhambra is the Alcázar or Casa Real (Royal Palace), mostly dating from the 14th century. Its survival is almost a miracle: the Christian conquerors neglected it; it was used for a while as a prison; and French troops looted it during the Napoleonic Wars.

Entering the palace complex through the former council cham- 27 ber *(Mexuar)* the first highlight is the Patio de los Arrayanes (Court of the Myrtle Trees), with two parallel hedges bordering a reflecting pool where red and gold carp slowly drift. Leading off it is perhaps the most beautiful room in the Alhambra, the Hall of the Ambassadors *(Salón de Embajadores)*, with a ceiling of carved cedar 18 m (60 ft) high. The walls are covered with finely carved Arabic script and shimmering tiles.

Another exit from the Court of the Myrtle Trees passes through a forest of slim columns into the Patio de los Leones (Lions' Courtyard), where a dozen stone lions support a splashing fountain. (Water in abundance, ingeniously diverted from the River Darro, is a repeated motif in the Alhambra.) Around this courtyard are more extraordinary rooms. The Hall of the two Sisters has an elaborately sculpted stalactitic ceiling; nearby steps lead down to the baths. The Hall of the Kings has figurative paintings of Moorish and Christian kings, and other scenes, on the curved ceilings of three alcoves, half-hidden from view. It was against Islamic norms to show human or even animal figures in art, but the Nasrid kings of Granada wrote their own rules. The artists may have been Christians, and the position of the pictures meant that those who might be offended wouldn't have to see them.

After the Reconquest, part of the Alcázar was destroyed so that a palace could be built for Emperor Charles V. The solid, rather grim Palacio de Carlos V is entirely out of keeping with the delicate Moorish work, but a Renaissance monument nevertheless, although it was left unfinished. The circle-within-a-square design is credited to Pedro Machuca, a student of Michelangelo. Some of the rooms around the circular courtyard house the Museo Nacional de Arte Hispano-Musulmán (Hispano-Islamic Museum), with Moorish carving, stucco, ceramics and other work from the Alhambra and elsewhere. The Fine Arts Museum on the upper floors displays mainly religious paintings form the 16th to 19th centuries.

Generalife

Outside the walls of the Alhambra, a little way to the north on the same hill, are the gardens that once surrounded the Moorish kings' summer palace. Little remains of the buildings, but the formal gardens are superb, with terraces, fountains and flowers, bordered by stately avenues of evergreen trees. The name Generalife may be derived from the Arabic for "architect's garden".

The famous Patio of the Lions, in Granada's Alhambra palace.

Cathedral and Capilla Real

The massive cathedral was begun in 1521 and work continued for 200 years—hence the range of styles from Gothic to baroque—and it is still incomplete. The main chapel, Capilla Mayor, is a domed rotunda with a striking double row of upper windows. Otherwise the building is heavy, grey and depressing.

Much more appealing than the cathedral is the nearby Capilla Real (Royal Chapel), built by order of Ferdinand and Isabella to be their mausoleum. The sacristy houses some of the queen's collection of jewellery and paintings, including works by Botticelli, Memling and Van der Weyden (a Pietá and a Nativity), and various royal insignia. In the magnificently decorated chapel itself the Catholic Monarchs, their daughter Juana la Loca and her husband Felipe are honoured by white marble effigies behind an elaborate iron grille; they are actually interred in plain lead coffins visible in the crypt below.

In front of the cathedral is the old Arab silk market, the Alcaiceria, restored and full of souvenir shops. Make your way to nearby Plaza Bib Rambla, where you can sit at a tree-shaded terrace and observe the people of Granada at work and play.

29

COSTA DEL SOL
Almería, Almuñécar, Nerja, Málaga, Torremolinos, Fuengirola, Mijas, Marbella, Ronda, Estepona

Having reached your base on this holiday coast, it may be tempting to stay put, but when you feel like a change, you'll find the coastal towns are not all the same. The capital city of Málaga, far from being swamped by tourism, has a distinctly Spanish flavour. For variety, a short excursion inland from almost any point on the coast takes you to pretty villages and spectacular mountain scenery.

Almería

The eastern gateway to the Costa del Sol was once the Moors' chief port in Spain, and the last to fall, in 1488. Its name comes from the Arabic Al-Mariyya, "mirror of the sea", referring to the bright circle of its bay which reflects the almost constant sunshine.

The colour and hubbub of a working Mediterranean port fill the old town near the harbour, morning and evening. Ferries link it with Melilla, the smaller of the Spanish enclaves on the African coast, carrying many Moroccans to work in the greenhouses of the "sea of plastic" (see p. 31).

The tree-lined Paseo is a promenade for shoppers and strollers, with outdoor cafés offering a view of the changing scene for the price of a coffee or cool drink. The pace picks up at the time of the pre-dinner stroll, when it can seem as if half the population of 200,000 has turned out, to work up an appetite while seeing and being seen.

The winter climate is one of the best in Spain, attracting Scandinavians and other northerners for a break in the sun. To the west of Almería, Aguadulce and Roquetas de Mar are tourist resorts intended to rival the attractions of the Costa del Sol's big names.

The Old City

In the old quarter, the western area of the city, Almería's Gothic cathedral was begun in 1524. It has the look of a fortress, with round towers, bastions and crenellations: the architects had in mind the constant threat of raids by Barbary pirates. However, the interior decoration of the three naves is suitably grand. Other churches in the town are also worth a visit. San Juan was built on the site of a 10th-century mosque, and the *mihrab* or niche showing the direction of Mecca is still visible. In the sanctuary of Santo Domingo church is the Gothic sculpture of the Virgin of

THE SEA OF PLASTIC

Around the ancient port of Adra, founded by the Phoenicians, and all the way west to Motril, every available bit of land has been covered with plastic sheeting. Endless expanses of greenhouses allow growers to send Europe's earliest vegetables, salads, fruit and flowers to supply the markets of the cold north. The boom began when the chemical industry came up with inhibitors that stopped the plastic turning brittle in the sun, and really took off when modern fast roads were built across Spain.

the Sea, Almería's patroness; legend says the wooden statue was found floating in the bay in 1502.

Alcazaba

At the top of the town, the Alcazaba is the restored 10th century Moorish fortress. Its walls and turrets now surround peaceful parks and gardens, but in its heyday it could hold 20,000 defenders. It fell not to attack, but in the earthquakes of 1522 and 1560, and was abandoned until restoration was decreed in the Franco era. The La Chanca quarter, between the fortress and the sea, still looks like a North African town and preserves the Moorish street pattern.

Excursions

In the mountains to the north of Almería, the sparse rainfall and relentless sun combine to create a surreal semi-desert. Near Tabernas the dramatic scenery has been used by film companies as the setting for science fiction movies or as the "badlands" in Sergio Leone's westerns. Some of the film sets have been re-used as Mini-Hollywood, a tourist attraction featuring cowboys, rustlers, sheriffs, stunts and shoot-outs.

Pioneering work has been done here on solar power and the vegetation of arid lands, with reforestation projects on some slopes. Sorbas, 26 km (16 miles) beyond Tabernas, is a village known for its pottery. Its white houses, clinging to the edge of a ravine, seem suspended in air.

The coast east of Almería, protected as the Cabo de Gata Nature Park, has secluded coves, dramatic cliffs, and is a scuba diver's paradise.

Almuñécar

On the coast between Almería and Málaga, this town was founded by the Phoenicians, who named it Sexi. There is still a Phoenician necropolis, but the most interesting sights are around the Moorish castle and El Majuelo park in the old town. Unattractive buildings encircle the town, but the neighbouring 31 coastal landscape is spectacular, and inland tropical crops such as avocado and mangoes thrive.

Nerja

The biggest resort east of Málaga has managed to avoid the worst excesses of highrise building and other ugly effects of unrestrained expansion. There's no shortage of discos and bars, but the old centre still looks like the charming little fishing village it once was. The clifftop Balcón de Europa juts out to sea between two sheltered beaches; more beaches spread along the coast to the east.

Nerja Caves

Inland from Maro, about 6 km (4 miles) from Nerja, in 1959, some boys chasing bats discovered the entrance to a huge system of limestone caverns. These were quickly given protection, so they escaped the damage that some longer-known caves suffered from souvenir hunters. Large parts are still closed to the public, including areas with prehistoric rock paintings of deer, horses, goats, marine animals and figures of humans, or gods. From these and other evidence it seems that the caves were inhabited at various times between 20,000 and 1800 BC.

Visitors can see a series of chambers, well-lit and given fanciful names. The first displays archaeological finds and photos of the ancient art; then comes the Hall of Bethlehem, full of spectacularly beautiful stalactites and stalagmites. With a central cascade, the Hall of the Waterfall is the scene of ballet and concert performances during the annual Festival of the Caves in July. In the enormous Hall of the Cataclysm, so-called because fallen rocks suggest an earthquake long ago, a gigantic central column 32 m (105 ft) high rates as the tallest of its kind in the world. It was formed when, after hundreds of thousands of years of imperceptible growth, a stalactite and stalagmite finally met and joined.

Frigiliana

As pretty a village as you could hope to see stands on the hillside only 5 km (3 miles) inland from Nerja. With its clustered white buildings and narrow streets, the old village centre probably looks much as it did in Moorish times, although many of the houses have been bought by foreigners.

Málaga

The chief city of the Costa del Sol leads a double life, as a hardworking port and industrial centre, and the sunny gateway to one of Europe's prime resort areas. The historic heart of the city still carries the mark of almost eight centuries of Moorish rule. And if

ÁLAGA

300 m
300 yd

Parador
Nacional
de Gibralfaro

Paseo de Reding

Pl.
de Toros

Calle Cervantes

Maestranza

Av. Canovas del Castillo

Mar
Mediterránia

La Malagueta

Castillo
Gibralfaro

Comandancia
de Marina
O. Publicas

Paseo Marítimo

Pl.
Santa María

Pl.
Hospital
Noble

San Nicolas

Muelle Ricardo G. Onela

Paseo de la Farola

C. de los
Frailes

C. de la Vi...

La Alcazaba
(Museo
Arqueológico)

Teatro
Romano

G. Sotelo

Pl.
Merced

Santiago
el Mayor

Ayuntamiento

Puerto

de Dios

Calle Alamos

Calle Beatas

Museo de
Bellas Artes

Gobierno
Civil

Aduana

Paseo del Parque

Paseo de España

Muelle de Guadiaro

El Parque

Estación
Marítima

Calle Méndez Núñez

Pl. de la Granada

Granada

Cister

Catedral

Calle
Molina

Obispo

Pl. de

la Marina

S. Ignacio

Stos.
Mártires

Pl.
Constitución

Cisneros

Pl.
Flores

Calle Nueva

Martinez

Pl. de los
Marqués

Santo
Cristo

Pl.
San
Juan

Huerta
Gtez.

Arco de
Cabeza

Pta. Nueva

Córdoba

Calle Trinidad Grund

Muelle de Heredia

Muelle de Romero Robledo

Rosal

Avda. de

Camas

Tomás
Atarazanas
Panaderos

Calle Heredia

Calle de Vendeja

Calle de Campos

Puente
Aurora

Museo de
Arte y Tradiciones
Populares

Puente
S. Domingo

Mercado
Central

C. Heredia

Casas

Alameda

C. de S. Lorenzo

Mercado

Zamorano

A. de Bazán

Carretería

Carretería

S. Domingo

Puente de
Tetuán

Alameda de Colon

Duques de Parcent

Puente del
Carmen

Calle Marmoles

A. del Obispo

Esquilache

Río Guadalmedina

Comandante Benitez

Calle Marmoles

Calle
de la Puente

Almansa

Montes de la Mota

Puente del

Don Cristián

Avda.
Principal

San Pedro,
Museo de
Semana Santa

Avenida de la Aurora

Armengual de la Mota

N.S. del
Carmen

Arroya del Cuarto

Mar
Mediterránia

you arrive in spring for the Holy Week processions of hooded penitents and elaborate floats bearing sacred images, you might think little had changed since the 16th century.

Like most coastal cities in the region, Málaga was a Phoenician colony 3000 years ago, then part of the empires of Carthage and Rome. Taken by the Moors soon after they invaded in 711, it prospered as the port for Granada.

City Centre

Behind the modern port, built on land won from the sea, Paseo del Parque is a garden-lined avenue shaded by palms and plane trees.

Just inland of it stand the city's major monuments and the old quarter.

The flavour of Málaga, old and new, can be sampled along Calle de Granada, a pedestrian street, and the maze of neighbouring streets and alleys. *Tapas* bars serve the region's wines, and the investigation can continue in one of the *bodegas*, old-fashioned wine shops lined with casks—the traditional sweet wines of the area have been augmented by table wines in recent years. More local colour pervades the huge Mercado Central (Central Market), with its ornate horseshoe-shaped gate which was once part

---

THE PICASSO CONNECTION

Picasso was born in Málaga in 1881, in an apartment in the 19th-century Casas de Campo, facing Plaza de Merced. The building has been completely remodelled; the rooms where his family lived are now part of a study centre run by the Pablo Ruiz Picasso Foundation. A few of his sketches, etchings and ceramics are on display, with family photographs and memorabilia, but the main purpose of the place is to run a service to scholars and a specialized library on avant-garde art.

Picasso's father was an art teacher, and the boy's exceptional talent was quickly recognized. Although the family moved to Barcelona when he was 14, and he was soon afterwards drawn to the modernists' magnet, Paris, Málaga remains proud of its famous son (the airport is named after him), but until recently it possessed pathetically little of his work. Then in 1996, the artist's daughter-in law Christine agreed to present the city with over 130 of his paintings, sculptures and ceramics, from every period of his career, including portraits of his first wife, Olga Koklova, and son Paul (Christine's husband). They form the basis of a new Picasso Museum scheduled to open in 1999.

of the Moorish city walls. Stalls are laden with fruit and vegetables, fish and shellfish from tiny clams to giant swordfish, and the scents of herbs and spices are mouthwatering.

Horse-drawn carriages stand ready to take you sightseeing, but be sure to negotiate the price and the duration of the tour before you set off.

Alcazaba

On a hill next to the former shoreline, the Alcazaba is a rambling 15th-century fortress where the city's Moorish rulers lived. Facing the entrance is a restored section of the 1st century Roman theatre.

The Cathedral

In the heart of the older part of the city, the cathedral is an oddity. Although its Renaissance, baroque and neoclassical parts add up to a rather majestic ensemble, it has only one tower and the stump of a second, where work stalled more than 200 years ago through lack of money. Local people call it *La Manquita*, "the little one-armed lady". The treasures inside benefit from excellent lighting and really informative labelling in English, French and Spanish. There are fine carvings of saints in the choir, a Gothic altar in the Chapel of Santa Barbara, and a statue of the Virgin presented by

Ferdinand and Isabella when the city was captured from the Moors.

Gibralfaro

The high point of the city takes its name from *Jebel al Faro*, the Arabic for Hill of the Lighthouse. Reached by a winding road on its eastern side, the summit is crowned by restored Moorish ramparts on even older foundations. The panoramic view of the city, port and beaches is magnificent, and almost as good from the parador which stands just downhill from the top. Its gardens seem suspended like a balcony over the city and, at the foot of the hill, its instantly recognisable 19th-century bullring, also used for concerts. It is best to drive or take a taxi rather than walk to the top, as the thick pine forest on the slopes attracts Málaga's more unsavoury characters.

Inland Excursions

An hour's drive or a train ride from Málaga, Antequera is an attractive old town on the edge of a vast, fertile valley with a number of Roman sites. On the outskirts are some even older monuments, three Stone Age *dolmens*, burial chambers dating from about 2000 BC. The best preserved, the Dolmen de Menga, is like a spacious room with remarkably regular walls and a roof 35

From the top of Gibralfaro mountain, you can see all of Málaga and its port.

formed of massive capstones weighing up to 110 tonnes.

The national park of El Torcal is a high plateau of limestone carved by the elements into fantastic shapes—chasms, pinnacles and cliffs where great griffon vultures soar in the rising air currents.

El Chorro canyon near the town of Alora is a favourite picnic spot with local people. The Guadalhorce river which cut this prodigious gorge, 300 m (1000 ft) deep, has been dammed higher up to create some beautiful lakes. Instead of returning directly to the coast, it's possible to take little-used back roads to Ronda.

Torremolinos

The biggest and brashest of them all, this cheerful resort 15 km (9 miles) west of Málaga is unashamedly dedicated to fun. Historic monuments are thin on the ground, for Torremolinos was founded as a fishing village in the 19th century. The 9-km (6-mile) strip of beach brought the first wave of tourists in the 1950s, and then a flood which led to the whole seafront being built up with hotels and holiday apartments.

In high season, bodies pack the beach by day and the bars and discos by night. It's noisy and sweaty, but that's the way they like it. Beachfront cafés sell great fried fish, and pubs and restaurants cater to every national taste in beer and food—British, German, Swedish, Dutch and a dozen more. Unhappy with the downmarket image, the local authorities have improved beach cleaning and cracked down on noise and street crime. A conference centre a little way inland brings a more sober crowd, and outside the summer months the place is positively staid. As diversions, there are displays of Spanish horsemanship at the Riding Centre; you can take lessons yourself, and go trekking on horseback in the hills. Children can make a splash in the giant aquapark with its huge slides and wavepool.

Benalmádena-Costa

The resort to the west of Torremolinos used to be quite separate. Now they have joined up, but Benalmádena aspires to a touch more class. More typical facilities include a funfair with Wild West and flamenco shows, a casino and a yacht marina. The Sealife Centre features close encounters with sharks—you walk through a transparent tunnel surrounded by them. A few kilometres inland from the coast is the picturesque village of Benalmádena itself. Its Museum of Pre-Colombian Art from Mexico and Peru is one of the best of its kind in Spain.

Fuengirola

Fuengirola resembles a smaller Torremolinos, warts and all. But traditional life goes on. Ignoring the tourist crowd, the town's fishermen still put out to sea, and the Tuesday morning market is colourful enough to attract excursion parties from other resorts along the coast.

Mijas

The look of old Andalusia has been preserved in this village in the hills behind Fuengirola, though at peak times it can be swamped by holiday crowds. Whitewashed houses line charming streets where the traffic is restricted to pedestrians and donkeys acting as "taxis". Mijas has the country's only square-shaped bullring, with a small museum attached, and many souvenir shops and restaurants. In the upper town the streets turn into flights of steps and the higher you climb, the prettier it becomes, and the lower are the restaurant prices.

Marbella

A big, stylish resort with 28 km (17 miles) of beaches, Marbella regards itself as the aristocrat of the Costa del Sol, attracting the rich, the famous, and those who would like to be. Its name is attributed to Queen Isabella of Castile, who is supposed to have 37 remarked on the "beautiful sea" *(mar bella)*, but its origins go back to the Phoenicians, who called it Salduba (Salt City).

The seafront promenade is not so different from the other resorts on this coast. This is not where the super-rich are to be found, despite the helipad near the fishing port. They are secluded in their own villas or exclusive clubs, or aboard their private yachts.

Away from the hotels, marinas and beaches, north of the main coastal highway, is the Old Town with its narrow, winding streets. You can watch the passing scene from the cafés around Plaza de los Naranjos, faced by the stately white 16th-century Ayuntamiento (City Hall).

West of Marbella is the big marina of Puerto Banús, where some of the world's most expensive yachts are berthed. Elegant shops and restaurants meet the standards—and budgets—of their owners, but you don't have to be rich to stroll the quayside and gaze.

Ronda

Ronda can be reached by a narrow twisting road from Algeciras and Gibraltar, the last part through the bare limestone karst scenery of the Serranía de Ronda mountains, once a haunt of bandits. An easier, faster road from San Pedro de Alcántara on the coast near Marbella carries most of the tourist traffic.

The picturesque old town perches on a high spur of rock split by a vertigo-inducing ravine. Plunging to a depth of 150 m (nearly 500 ft) it separates La Ciudad, the old Moorish town on the south side, from the newer El Mercadillo (Little Market) district. Three bridges span the gorge: those with a head for heights will enjoy gazing down from the Puente Nuevo, the "new bridge" which was built in the 18th century. The two older bridges are at the lower end of the gorge. The 13th-century Moorish Baths *(Baños Arabes)*, close to the river, still preserve a large part of their vaulted roof.

4 FOUR PICTURESQUE VILLAGES The prettiest towns and villages, clusters of traditional white houses, are a little way inland. Make a diversion to see **Casares**, on a hilltop above Estepona; **Mijas**, on the terraced slopes behind Fuengirola; photogenic **Frigiliana**, close to Nerja; and **Vejer de la Frontera** above the Atlantic coast near Cape Trafalgar.

La Ciudad

The older part of the city retains much of its Moorish atmosphere. Isolation and bristling fortifications kept it in Muslim hands until very late in the process of Christian Reconquest; it fell at last to an overwhelming force in 1485. The Palacio de Mondragón, built by a ruler of Ronda in 1314, became a summer residence of Spanish monarchs. The mood is set by courtyards and gardens, full of scented flowers and the sound of running water, with a stirring view from the cliff-top terrace. The palace houses a small, informative museum, with displays on prehistory, Moorish art, crafts and architecture.

The Church of Santa María la Mayor was built on the site of Ronda's principal mosque and made use of some of its features: the minaret became a bell tower, and two arches, the *mihrab* and several domes also survive from the earlier building. Inside, there is a beautifully carved baroque choir stall, and an ornate high altar.

El Mercadillo

Facing the gorge and the Puente Nuevo on the north side, a new parador has been built, carefully matching the arcaded stonework of its neighbours.

The Plaza de Toros (1785) is claimed to be the oldest bullring in Spain. In this neoclassical arena with its elegant two-storey arcade, the celebrated Pedro Romero (1754–1838) was the first to elaborate the rules of bull-fighting. His grandfather Francisco Romero had already introduced the cape and *muleta* into the ritual.

Estepona

A pleasantly old-fashioned resort with a palm-fringed promenade, Estepona is also a traditional Spanish working town and fishing port. Just a couple of streets away from the beach, the old centre seems to live a completely separate life.

Inland, 14 km (9 miles) up a wooded valley, reached by a narrow, twisting road, Casares is one of the most photogenic of the "white towns" *(pueblos blancos)* of the region.

Sotogrande

Lacking large beaches, the coast to the west of Estepona was late into the leisure business. When development came, it was carefully planned and aimed at the luxury end of the market. Golf was the spur: the Valderrama course is rated one of the most beautiful in Europe. It was chosen as the venue for the 1997 Ryder Cup, the first time the event had been held outside Britain or the US.

COSTA DE LA LUZ
Tarifa, Vejer de la Frontera, Cádiz,
Sanlúcar de Barrameda, Jerez de la Frontera

Breezier, with tide-washed expanses of sand facing the Atlantic, the southwest coast of Spain is far less developed than the Costa del Sol. The wind and the waves may have deterred early developers; now they attract windsurfers. The ancient port of Cádiz is off the usual tourist track and well worth a detour. Jerez de la Frontera is the historic centre of the sherry trade, and equally devoted to its horses.

Tarifa
The southernmost tip of Spain and nearest point to Africa looks across at the mountainous coast of Morocco, a mere 15 km (9 miles) away. Ferries link it to Tangier. Such a strategic position at the entrance to the Mediterranean meant that Tarifa was often besieged. The Moorish castle and town walls have been restored; Isla de las Palomas, an islet reached by a sand-blown causeway, is encrusted with fortifications and is still a military base.

Hundreds of wind-powered generators built on the highest points of the ridges inland extract energy from the strong winds that blow through the straits. Down on Tarifa's beaches, the world's best windsurfers gather to exploit the same power source, skimming across the waves and performing spectacular aerobatics.

Near Bolonia, 12 km (7 miles) to the west, a minor road down to the sea (7 km) leads to an important Roman site, the ruins of Baelo Claudia. Excavation is still going on, but the outlines of temples, the forum, marketplace and basilica can be seen.

Vejer de la Frontera
Just off the main road to Cádiz is the ultimate in white hilltop towns. Its sleepy maze of steep, twisting streets and little box-like houses climbs to a Moorish castle and Gothic church. Magnificent views down to the sea take in Cape Trafalgar, which gave its name to the 1805 battle fought off this coast.

Barbate is a brash, noisy, very Spanish seaside resort—soccer on the sand, grandmas dipping their toes in the water, teenagers showing off and excellent fish restaurants.

Cádiz
Although legend credits the foundation of Cádiz to Hercules, it was probably the Phoenicians who spotted the excellent harbour

Windsurf fanatics from all over Europe come to ride the waves at Tarifa.

and established a trading post around 1100 BC. Their successors the Carthaginians took over in 501 BC. The settlement prospered under the Romans; Julius Caesar awarded its people Roman citizenship. The Moors showed less interest and Cádiz was almost depopulated when it was taken from them in 1262 during the Christian Reconquest.

The port reached a pinnacle of fame and fortune as a result of trade with the Spanish possessions in the Americas. Such wealth attracted attacks from North African Barbary pirates as well as English raiders, including among their ranks Sir Francis Drake (himself regarded as no better than a pirate by the Spanish), who "singed the King of Spain's beard" by burning some ships in a 1587 raid. As Seville's port silted up, Cádiz took over as headquarters of the New World Fleet in 1680.

During the Napoleonic Wars, Spanish ships fought alongside the French fleet at the Battle of Trafalgar (1805), off the coast to the south of Cádiz. The survivors limped into port there after the battle. When France later invaded Spain and besieged the city in 1810, it was eventually relieved by Wellington's army. During the siege, the Cortes (parliament) had 41

CÁDIZ

assembled in Cádiz and drawn up a liberal constitution, although this was abolished when Ferdinand VII regained his throne in 1814.

Almost completely surrounded by water, Cádiz stands at the end of an 8-km (5-mile) strip of salt marshes edged by sand beaches. The port facing the sheltered bay is the home of a fishing fleet, and ferries sail to the Canary Islands and Morocco. The newer part of the city has spread back along the peninsula, leaving the charming old centre little touched by modernity.

The Old City

Historic Cádiz is still almost encircled by its fortifications, a series of bastions and walls facing the sea. Its main gates lead into an irregular maze of narrow streets, thronged morning and late into the evening, bathed in a haunting silence during the long siesta. Dark alleys, lined by tall whitewashed houses and old churches, open suddenly into squares shaded by palm trees. As darkness falls, restaurant tables take over some of the streets and squares; at fiesta time they become informal stages for dancers and musicians.

In the middle of the narrow neck of land between the port and the sea, Plaza de San Juan de Dios is the biggest and liveliest of many squares. On the waterfront facing the port, a former tobacco factory built of patterned brick in Moorish style is now a convention centre.

To the west of the plaza, next to the sea, the enormous cathedral was built between 1702 and 1838. Its white limestone glistens in the sun, but salt spray from the sea has caused alarming erosion. Inside, all is high baroque, with elaborate stonework, carved choirstalls, gilded altars and collections of gold and silver. The Cádiz-born composer Manuel de Falla is buried in the crypt. Still called *Catedral Nueva*—the New Cathedral—it took over from the church of Santa Cruz, *Catedral Vieja*, which almost adjoins it. Even more fortress-like, this dates from the 13th century but had to be rebuilt after an English raid in 1596. Below its walls, the foundations and lower seat rows of a Roman theatre have been uncovered.

The 18th-century Santa Cueva chapel, in Calle Rosario, has three paintings by Goya on the walls of its oval interior, and the Hospital de Nuestra Señora del Carmen (or Hospital de Mujeres) has a fine El Greco of St Francis.

Cádiz Museum

In Plaza de Mina on the north side of town, the museum concentrates on two topics, Archae- 43 ology and Fine Art. On the ground floor, the archaeological section begins with fine prehistoric flints and bronze jewellery and tools. Objects from local Phoenician and Roman burial sites include huge sarcophagi in human shape. Most eyecatching are the magnificent statues of emperors and gods.

Upstairs are the Fine Art galleries, mostly Spanish painting from the 16th to the 20th centuries. The many pictures by Zurbarán include a set of saints from the Cartuja at Jerez. Several works by Murillo lead up to one giant creation, The *Mystic Marriage of Santa Catarina*, which cost the artist his life. While working on it, he fell from a platform and later died from his injuries. The painting was finished by one of his students. Flemish and Italian 17th-century pictures widen the scope beyond Spain. Miró is the best-known of the 20th-century Spanish painters represented.

The Tourist Information Office is nearby at the north corner of the same square.

Cádiz Bay

The broad blue expanse of the Bay of Cádiz is the venue for many sailing events, and its beaches are more sheltered than those facing the open sea. Two of its ports are popular resorts.

El Puerto de Santa María

Across the bay from Cádiz at the mouth of the River Guadalete, El Puerto ("the port") shipped most of the sherry from Jerez until modern container methods took over. Some of the town's *bodegas*, such as Osborne, Terry and Duff Gordon still offer tastings, and the shellfish and fried fish restaurants are renowned. With sandy beaches, a casino, marina and huge bullring, the old port is a local family favourite.

Sanlúcar de Barrameda

The old port at the mouth of the Guadalquivir saw Columbus embark on his last voyage to the Americas in 1498, and Magellan leave with his five ships in 1519. Only one returned, three years later, with the 18 survivors who had achieved the first circumnavigation of the world. The 14th-century church of Santa María was built by Mudéjar artisans after the Reconquest, using the same techniques and some of the designs they might have employed on a mosque.

Sanlúcar is a sherry producer, though not on the scale of Jerez. The wine made here is *manzanilla*, dry, crisp and better-known these days in Spain than abroad. A newer industry is the greenhouse production of flowers and other early crops; huge refrigerated trucks wait to load up and head for northern Europe. Look for signposts to the flower market on the edge of town—visitors are welcome.

Buyers come from Seville and Córdoba to Sanlúcar's fish market, and diners are attracted from Cádiz and Jerez to the seafood restaurants which line Bajo de Guía on the banks of the Guadalquivir.

Doñana Nature Reserve

Across the river from Sanlúcar is a vast stretch of primeval landscape of a type which has all but vanished from the rest of Europe. (The Camargue in southern France is one of the few similar areas.) At first sight flat and almost featureless, it is actually a mosaic of different fragile environments: sand dunes, scrub, pine woods, stands of gnarled old cork-oak trees, and especially the marshes themselves, Las Marismas del Guadalquivir. In winter and spring they are classic wetlands, alive with thousands of waterfowl, including huge numbers of visiting wild geese from northwest Europe. Many other species nest here, moving on in summer when the marsh dries up. Deer, otters, wild boar and the rare lynx live in the reserve.

Access to the park is restricted, but visits can be arranged through tourist offices; morning and afternoon tours start at El Acebuche. One comfortable way to see the reserve is from the river boat which leaves from Bajo de Guía in Sanlúcar.

Jerez de la Frontera

This city of 170,000 is best known for its sherry wine, and is also Spain's major producer of brandy, which they sometimes call *coñac* to the despair of the French. The grape harvest is celebrated in September, with processions, women in traditional flounced dresses, and carts bearing an offering of grapes. At the steps of the cathedral, men tread the grapes in the old way, with

5 FIVE GREAT VIEWS Southern Iberia specializes in lookout points. Some of the best panoramas: **Málaga** from the Gibralfaro (or the parador); **Ronda** from the bridge over its vertiginous gorge; **Gibraltar** from the Top of the Rock; **Granada** and the Alhambra from the Mirador de San Nicolás in the Albaicín quarter; and the bird's eye view of **Seville** from the Giralda, once a Moorish minaret.

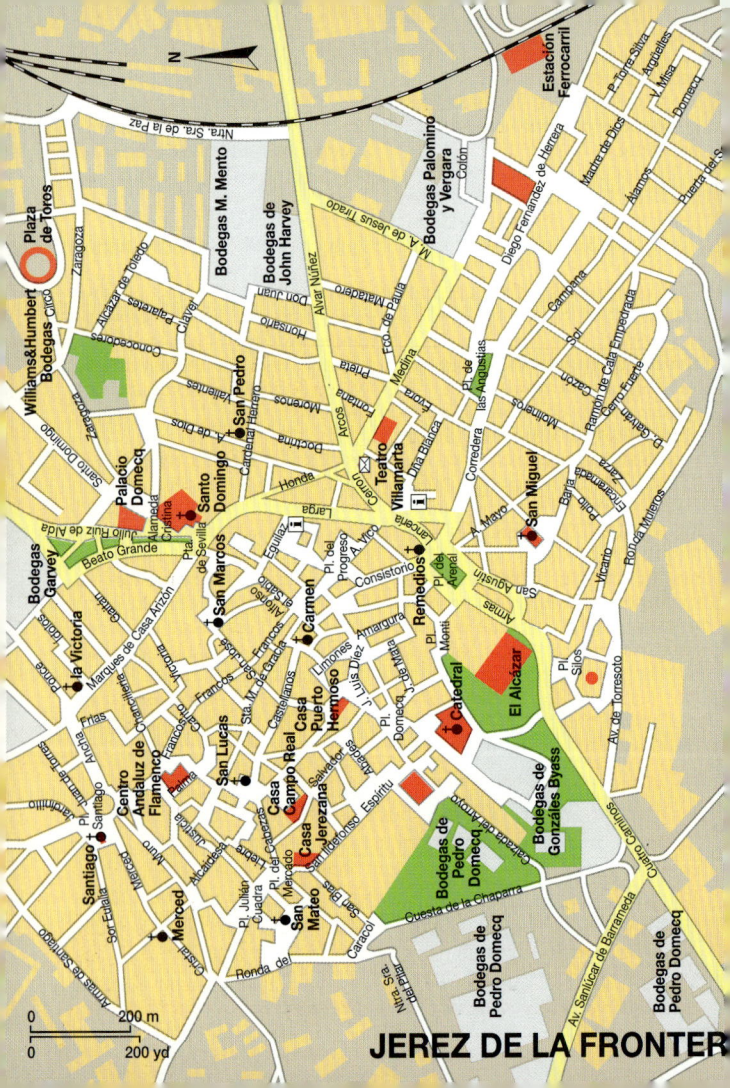

N

Estación
Ferrocarril

Bodegas Palomino
y Vergara

Williams&Humbert
Bodegas Circo

Plaza
de Toros

Bodegas M. Mento

Bodegas de
John Harvey

Palacio
Domecq

Santo
Domingo

San Pedro

Teatro
Villamarta

San Miguel

Bodegas
Garvey

San Marcos

Carmen

Remedios

Catedral

El Alcázar

La Victoria

San Lucas

Casa
Campo Real

Casa
Puerto
Hermoso

Bodegas de
Gonzáles Byass

Centro
Andaluz de
Flamenco

Casa
Jerezana

Santiago

Merced

San
Mateo

Bodegas de
Pedro Domecq

Bodegas de
Pedro Domecq

Bodegas de
Pedro Domecq

200 m

200 yd

JEREZ DE LA FRONTER

spiked boots, to release the juice without crushing the bitter pips. (Commercial pressing is entirely mechanized.)

Horsemanship is the city's other passion. Jerez is the centre of a horse-breeding region, with a famous horse show every May, and an International Horse Fair in October, when a thousand or more riders parade and compete in races and dressage.

Wine-making in the area could date back 3000 years to the Phoenicians, who are thought to have introduced the art from the eastern Mediterranean. (The name of their settlement, Xera, became Xeres—hence the word sherry—and then Jerez.) It was well established under the Romans: wine exports to Rome were of such good quality that Italian growers could not compete and in AD 92, Emperor Domitian ordered the destruction of Spanish vineyards. Fortunately this was not carried out.

The Sherry Houses

Dozens of famous producers are based in Jerez, among them Domecq, Williams and Humbert, González Byass and Croft. Over 700,000 butts of sherry, each containing 500 litres, and as many of brandy are stored in their *bodegas*. To transate the word as "cellar" scarcely does them justice— some are more like cathedrals.

One of Domecq's is inspired by the Great Mosque of Córdoba, and a great cast-iron dome at González Byass was designed by Eiffel, long before the Tower brought him fame.

The *bodegas* are spread around the city—the Tourist Office in Calle Larga can provide maps and information. For a small charge, most of the bigger companies welcome visitors on tours of their facilities. Multi-lingual guides explain the processes of pressing the grapes, fermentation, ageing and blending. Some of the butts on show are reserved for royalty, others have been signed by famous visitors, from opera singers to racing drivers.

After the tour, there are various types of wine to be sampled, and somehow they seem to taste much better than any sherry you ever had elsewhere. Naturally there is an opportunity to buy some bottles, T-shirts and other souvenirs in the *bodega* shop.

The Old City

The dark stone cathedral was built in the 17th and 18th centuries on the site of the city's biggest mosque, with an elaborately carved doorway. Inside is a precious image known as the Christ of the Vineyards. On a hill above the cathedral are the walls of the 12th-century Moorish alcázar, surrounded by gardens. Not 47 much is left of the interior of the palace apart from its chapel, converted from a small mosque.

To learn about flamenco, call in at the Flamenco Centre *(Cen-* *tro Andaluz de Flamenco)*, in an old palace. They show a video every hour, and can help you to track down authentic performances.

SHERRY

Baking hot summers and soil made up mainly of chalk might seem an unlikely recipe, yet the low hills near the mouth of the Guadalquivir produce Spain's most famous wine. As old sayings and modern science agree, harsh conditions can make for finer wines than rich earth and regular rain. Only one area can call its product sherry, that lying between Jerez de la Frontera, which gave sherry its name, and the port of Sanlúcar de Barrameda, which produces the variety known as *manzanilla*.

Called "sack" in England in the Middle Ages, and mentioned by Shakespeare, it became more widely known when hundreds of barrels were seized by Drake in his raid on Cádiz in 1587. Peace with Spain put exports on a more conventional footing, and English and Irish merchants moved to Jerez to found the famous sherry dynasties.

Sherry's character results from the unique *solera* system used to blend it. Rows of 500-litre oak butts are arranged in tiers or "scales" in the bodegas, the youngest wine in the top tier, the oldest in the lowest. Wine for bottling and shipping is taken only from the lowest butts, and not more than one-third of the contents of each, which is then topped up from the level above. Thus there are no vintages in sherry: the lowermost butts (and the bottles) will contain some wine from all the years when wine was added to them. Theoretically there will be traces from every year since the *solera* was started, in some cases over 150 years ago.

Most sherry is slightly fortified, by the addition of small amounts of grape alcohol, to stabilize it during ageing and shipping. Formerly Europe's (especially Britain's) preferred apéritif, it has lost ground to unfortified wines. But in its home territory, there can be no better pairing than a *copita* of cool, dry fino or *manzanilla* with a serving or two of *tapas*. The slightly darker, nutty *amontillado* and the richer *oloroso* (naturally dry, but usually sweetened by the addition of sweet wines) are the other main varieties.

Superimposed rows of barrels at the Gonzalez Byass winery in Jerez. The lowest rows contain the oldest sherry blends.

The Royal Riding School

Horse lovers will want to see a performance in the equestrian school, Real Escuela Andaluza del Arte Ecuestre, where the big *manège* or exercise hall was designed by Charles Garnier, architect of the Paris Opéra. The main shows are held on Thursdays at noon (there are additional performances in summer), but it's also possible to see the horses dance and prance at rehearsals on other days, between 11 a.m. and 1 p.m.

Carriages drawn by beautifully decorated teams of horses are sometimes seen practising in the neighbouring streets.

La Cartuja

Outside Jerez, 5 km (3 miles) to the southeast towards Medina Sidonia, La Cartuja is a restored 15th-century Carthusian monastery with a baroque façade of splendidly carved stone. This was where the Carthusian breed of horse was developed, and although the monastery was abandoned for centuries, a few monks are now back in residence, and visitors have to be content with seeing the façade and the garden in front of it. The exception: on Wednesdays and Saturdays, between 5 and 6 p.m., male visitors (only) are allowed to enter the church.

49

CULTURAL NOTES

Flamenco. Derived from gypsy, Moorish and even earlier roots, flamenco flowered in Andalusia. The rhythms of its songs and dances have influenced all Spanish music, but the hot-blooded south is their stamping ground.

Flamenco music comes in two distinct varieties. The soulful *cante jondo* (deep song) is an intensely dramatic outpouring of emotion, on the subjects of love, loss, anguish and death. In contrast, *cante chico* (light song) is fast, humorous and lively, on themes of happiness and the carefree country life.

In flamenco dances, the men make intricate steps, with rapid staccato heel-drumming and toe-tapping called *zapateado*, accompanied by a rhythmic snapping of the fingers, while women make graceful movements of the hands and body, with less detailed footwork. Men wear the slim Cordoban suit, and women the sweeping, ruffled gypsy-style dresses that have become the hallmark of flamenco.

Music is provided by guitars, often played with great virtuosity, echoing the steps of the dancer. Audiences respond with hand-clapping and enthusiastic shouts of approval.

Fiestas. Almost any time of the year, Andalusians will find an excuse to celebrate. An ancient battle, the harvest season, the feast day of a patron saint... any occasion is good for a *fiesta*. Each city and village has an annual *feria* (fair)—the most famous are Seville's in April and Málaga's in August—in which parading horses, flamenco, food and wine are key ingredients. Cádiz holds a carnival in late winter, Jerez stages a horse fair in May and wine harvest fair in Autumn, Córdoba celebrates is famous patios in May. The spring pilgrimage of El Rocío near the Doñana Nature Reserve attracts a million participants. Seaside towns honour their patroness, the Virgen del Carmen, with seaborne processions in mid-July. A fiesta is a good occasion to get to know the Andalusians at their best.

The religious festival of Holy Week is different in flavour. *Semana Santa*, the week leading up to Easter, is celebrated throughout Spain, but nowhere with greater passion than in Andalusia. Perhaps because the Christian Reconquest came to it later, the people have felt driven to parade their faith with maximum fervour.

In the cities, every parish church brings out its statue of the Virgin and Christ and carries them in procession through the streets. Elaborate floats, some borne on the backs of men, carry realistic, life-size scenes, from the Last Supper to the Crucifixion and Descent from the Cross. Penitents provide an escort, clad in long robes and pointed hoods with eye-slits, sinister echoes of the Inquisition. In Seville on Palm Sunday, and the Wednesday, Thursday and Friday of Holy Week, a dozen such throngs may converge on the Cathedral, watched by their parishioners and serenaded with hymns.

In Granada, women dressed all in black, with black mantilla shawls, join the processions. Good Friday in Córdoba is marked by mass in the cathedral within La Mezquita, the former mosque.

The Bullfight. Andalusia is the home of the bullfight, the *fiesta brava*, Spain's national spectacle. The season begins immediately after Easter and runs until October.

Man against bull, intelligence against instinct, brain against half a ton of potentially deadly brawn—for the bull the outcome is certain; for the matador

less so. You may not like what you see. You may swear never to go to a bullfight again. Or you may become a life-long aficionado. A display of artistry and courage, or the cruel torture, humiliation and slaughter of an innocent, ignorant creature? Perhaps it's both.

The bull has been bred to fight in the ring, and the *corrida* is a ritualized preparation for the bull's death. The fight is divided into *tercios*, or thirds, each act designed to further tire the bull. First the bull charges into the ring, and helpers play it with capes. Then the matador takes over, using the big red and yellow *capote*.

During the second *tercio* the *picador*, the mounted spearman, uses his lance on the bull's huge shoulder muscles, and the *banderilleros* place darts in the bull's shoulder.

In the third *tercio* the matador plays the bull with the small, dark red *muleta*, dominating the animal to the point when he can turn his back and casually walk away. In the "moment of truth", he lunges with his sword, aiming for a pin-point thrust between the shoulder blades which should kill the bull within seconds. Depending on his skill and bravery, the matador is awarded an ear, two ears or perhaps even the tail.

Shopping

Southern Spain inherited a craft tradition from the Moors, whose influence still shows in carpet-weaving, decorative tooling on leather, inlaid wood and metal work and the intricate arabesque designs of some ceramic tiles. By contrast, there's a wild profusion of often amusing souvenirs—bullfight posters with your name, flamenco dolls, wine skins, plastic castanets and miniature guitars.

Hours

Shops open at around 9.30 or 10 a.m. Most of them close at 1.30 or 2 p.m. for the long lunch-and-siesta break, re-opening at 4.30 or 5 p.m. and finally closing at about 7.30 or 8 p.m. Big stores in the cities may stay open throughout the day.

Where to Shop

The beach resorts naturally have plenty of souvenirs, but for regular shopping the selection is better and the prices are lower in working cities such as Málaga, Cádiz and Seville. There, too, you can find branches of the big department stores. For the latest in expensive fashion, take a look at the boutiques of Puerto Banús, near Marbella.

The cities have their markets, open every day except Sunday, and smaller towns have a street market the same day each week: for example on Monday in Marbella, Tuesday in Fuengirola and Nerja, Wednesday in Estepona, Thursday in Torremolinos and Friday in Benalmádena.

Ceramics

The legacy of the Moors is still evident in the range of decorative tiles *(azulejos)* you can find, many of them in the traditional geometric, arabesque, designs. A single tile can stand alone as an artwork, or a group form a picture.

Simple brown-glazed kitchen ware and charming hand-painted pottery in floral designs are made in many places. More specialized potters work in Córdoba, Granada and Sorbas, near Almería.

Metalwork

Lamps and candlesticks of hand-beaten copper and brass recall the Moorish past and are reasonably portable. Simpler designs are made from wrought iron—a weathervane might not be too heavy to take home.

Jewellery

Delicate filigree silver is particularly associated with Córdoba, but jewellers everywhere produce rings, bracelets, brooches and necklaces in traditional and modern designs. The artificial pearls made in Majorca are used in many attractive ways.

Leather

Boots of Spanish leather have been known for their quality for centuries, and today the range of leather goods is enormous. Men's and women's shoes, belts and handbags are well made and reasonably priced, and suede gloves and clothes are stylish. Specialist stores sell everything equestrian: saddles, harnesses and superb boots.

Weaving and Embroidery

The locally made rugs are attractive, especially from the Granada area and the Alpujarra valley south of the Sierra Nevada. Some stores will take orders for rugs and cushion covers to your own specification. Women working at home still produce intricate lace shawls (mantillas), embroidered handkerchiefs and bed linen—look for them in markets as well as shops, and compare prices.

Woodwork and Basketry

Salad bowls and servers, pepper mills and carvings are made from olive and other woods. Inlaid wooden chessboards are set with carved pieces in the form of Moorish and Christian kings, queens, knights and soldiers.

Woven baskets come in every shape and size, in wickerwork, reed and straw. Prices are much more reasonable at local markets than in souvenir shops.

Old and New

Unusual bygones turn up on market stalls although there are few bargains to be found these days. Antique dealers in particular know what they have, and add a premium if they are in tourist areas such as Ronda or the Barrio de Santa Cruz in Seville. Ancient keys, tiles, prints and woodcarvings can be attractive, but only an expert can tell if they are really old.

Food and Drink

Sherry, brandy, the local gin if you have a taste for it, wines, olive oil, Andalusian honey and big green or pungent dark olives, spices and nuts are worth buying to take home. Depending on the length of journey and import restrictions at your destination, carry some fresh or dried fruits and flowers, as gifts or just for yourself.

53

Dining Out

Andalusia is the home of gazpacho and sangría, the chilled soup and red wine punch that have spread to the rest of Spain and beyond. Sherry from Jerez tastes its best on its own ground. It makes an ideal partner for tapas, the bite-sized appetizers which fill the spaces before lunch or dinner.

Timing

Spanish people rarely think about lunch before 2 p.m. and typically sit down to dinner at 9.30 or 10 p.m., or even later. Visitors who can't wait that long need not worry. *Tapas* bars and cafeterias allow you to snack between meals. In any case, restaurants in resort areas have long since become used to foreign ways, opening by 1 p.m. for lunch and 8 or earlier for dinner. And cafeterias (either *auto-servicio*, self-service, or table service) are open for meals all day, and often late at night.

Breakfast

Holiday hotels may provide a buffet of fruits, cereals, cheeses, cold meats and hot dishes, enough to keep hunger at bay all day. And cafés in the resorts offer "traditional English" breakfasts.

Tapas

At bar counters, tasty morsels of food used to be served free with drinks, often on a little cover on top of the glass (*tapa* means "lid"). Now, you almost always have to pay, from 100 to 500 ptas, and more for rare delicacies. Some of the popular items are lined up on the bar, and a menu may be displayed listing the full selection. The choice might range from salted nuts and crisps to juicy green and black olives, stewed baby octopus, potato and onion omelette to spicy *chorizo* sausage, salami, air-cured ham (*jamón serrano*), snails, grilled prawns with garlic, tuna salad, cod's roe, clams or mussels.

It's easy to make a meal of *tapas*, especially if you ask for a larger portion, called a *ración*. The bar staff will keep a tally of what you have had, often by making chalk marks on the counter.

Soups

Gazpacho has spread to the rest of Spain and beyond, but you should be able to find an authentic version in Andalusia. In fact it's a liquid salad, a chilled purée of tomato, cucumber, green pepper, onion and garlic, with oil, vinegar and perhaps fried croutons. A Málaga variation is *ajo blanco* (white garlic), based on crushed almonds, garlic (naturally) with a garnish of grapes. *Sopa de pescado* and *sopa de mariscos* are hot and spicy, with tasty morsels of fish and shellfish.

Fish and Seafood

The Andalusians' own favourite food is a simple plateful of fried fish, so fresh, delicate and lightly fried that it's easy to understand their preference. Fresh anchovies *(boquerones)* and baby squid *(chopitos)* are two fried favourites. Hake *(merluza)*, sea bream *(besugo)*, swordfish *(pez espada)*, and sole *(lenguado)* are frequently available, and *fritura mixta* or *fritura malagueña* is a mixture, on the menu in many a seaside restaurant. Shellfish *(mariscos)* includes prawns *(gambas)*, squid *(calamares)*, small clams *(almejas)* and mussels *(mejillones)*.

Shellfish is usually a component of *paella*, a dish that has migrated down the coast from Valencia. Based on rice and saffron, paella traditionally contained rabbit, snails and eels, but these days other ingredients are more common: clams, mussels, prawns, chicken, red peppers and sundry vegetables.

Meats

Steakhouses and barbecues produce tasty grilled meats; the local pork and chicken can be excellent. *Riñones al Jerez* (kidneys sautéed in sherry) is a typical Andalusian dish—small portions often feature on a *tapas* counter. Rabbit and baby kid are featured in some country restaurants.

Desserts

Waiters will suggest a *postre* when they clear your main course, but the choice is limited: ice creams and sorbets, lemon tart, sweet pastries, fresh fruit and invariably *flan* (cream caramel).

Drinks

The many varieties of sherry are the best-known of the region's wines, but those from Montilla-Moriles, in the hills south of Córdoba, are quite similar. Málaga has made sweet, dark dessert wines since Roman times. Andalusia makes dry table wines too, but wine lists are dominated by more distinguished and reliable names from northern Spain, such as Rioja. The Jerez region makes as much brandy as sherry.

Sangría, that ice-cool blend of red wine, brandy and slices of lemon and orange, is as good (or bad) as its ingredients. Local and imported beers, soft drinks and fresh fruit juices are universal thirst-quenchers.

Sports

The sea is warm enough for swimming much of the year, and is the best place to cool off in the heat of summer. Equipment for all the water sports is available at the big resorts, practically every beach has someone renting out windsurfers, sailing dinghies, catamarans or pedalos, and you can water-ski, para-sail and scuba-dive. Land-based activities are on the increase: as well as tennis and golf, more and more people go cycling, pony-trekking and hiking through the mountains.

Water Sports

The almost tideless, usually calm Mediterranean makes the Costa del Sol a good place for beginners to learn to sail or windsurf. Conditions can be a lot more challenging along the breezier Costa de la Luz, where surfers ride the Atlantic rollers. Windiest of all is Tarifa, at the southernmost tip of Spain, venue of international windsurfing competitions.

The sea west of Málaga often isn't clear enough to be ideal for snorkelling and scuba-diving—the best conditions are off the rocky shores east of Almería. Many resorts have diving clubs offering tuition and equipment rental.

Marinas all along the Costa del Sol, at Gibraltar and on the Bay of Cádiz provide berths for visiting yachts, and crewed and bareboat charter can be arranged.

Fishing

Local people fish from every rock, breakwater and bridge and you are welcome to join them. Boats for sport fishing offshore can be hired at marinas, complete with an expert captain to guide you to right place to catch a tuna or shark. No licence is needed for fishing in the sea, but you do need one for the rivers and lakes—ask at local tourist offices.

Hiking

An informal walk in the hills is a special pleasure in springtime, for example in the national parks near Antequera, inland from Málaga. Organized treks in the Sierra Nevada and other scenic areas are a way to get off the usual routes. On more expensive walking tours, a van takes your baggage between overnight stops at hotels or hostels.

Horse-riding

Andalusia takes great pride in its horses and its horsemanship. Most of the resorts of the Costa del Sol have a riding stable where you can hire a horse, join a trek in the hills or go for an early morning canter along a beach. Equestrian enthusiasts can take lessons in dressage and other skills at the riding schools of Seville, Jerez and Arcos de la Frontera.

Tennis and Squash

Resort hotels and clubs usually have several tennis courts, some with floodlighting for play in the cooler conditions of evening. Famous players have lent their names to tennis centres offering intensive coaching, which can be part of a holiday package. Squash courts are among the facilities at the more elaborate resort complexes and clubs.

Golf

Plenty of visitors head for southern Spain with no intention of going near the beaches. Golf is their game, and they are well provided with courses. Sotogrande, near Gibraltar, is a resort dedicated to golf; its Valderrama course designed by Robert Trent Jones was the venue for the Ryder Cup in 1997. The Costa del Sol has more than thirty courses, and there are more near Jerez, Cádiz and Seville. Some

are attached to hotels, others are private clubs, but most welcome non-members although they usually give reservation preference to members. Equipment can usually be hired, and tuition is often available.

Skiing

Snowcapped for much of the year, the Sierra Nevada began to attract skiers looking for an alternative to the Alps. Now they have the Solynieve resort, near the 3,398-m (11,148-ft) summit of the Veleta peak, controversially but beautifully situated in a national park. In a good year, the season can stretch into May.

Spectator Sports

Futbol (soccer) is *numero uno* in the affections of Spain's sports fans, with practically the status of a religion. If Andalusia's own teams are not exactly in the top class, no matter. The supporters get vicarious thrills by following the fortunes of the likes of Réal Madrid or Barcelona. Matches, on Sundays and weekday evenings, keep them glued to the TV, preferably in their favourite bar, and highlights are endlessly replayed and debated.

Bullfighting is more a ritual than a sport. It has long since been overtaken by football, but remains popular and commands a lot of TV time.

The Hard Facts

To help you plan your trip, here are some of the practical details you should know about Andalusia.

Airports

Málaga's busy international airport is located midway between the city and Torremolinos. Buses and trains run to Málaga and the nearby resorts, at 30-minute intervals throughout the day. Taxis are available at any time.

Seville and Jerez de la Frontera are served by flights from many European cities, mostly via Madrid. Gibraltar is a hub for British Airways flights operated by GB Airways, with daily nonstop services to and from London, both Heathrow and Gatwick.

Baggage

On most flights, the allowance for check-in baggage is 20 kg (44 lb). One small carry-on bag is permitted.

Car Rental

Hiring a car is a convenient and fairly economical way of getting around. Some of the international companies are represented in Spain, and it may be worth making a reservation through one of them in your home country, before your visit. Good local companies also operate from airports, major cities and resorts, but whichever you use, check that rates include full insurance against loss and damage, and local taxes. There is usually no limit on the distance you can cover, but an extra charge may be levied for drop-off at a different location, and for additional driver(s).

To rent a car, you need a current driving licence and to be aged over 21 (25 with some companies). You are expected to pay with a major credit card.

Climate

Summers are hot and dry. Daytime temperatures inland can be over 40°C (104°F); sea breezes make the coasts less torrid. Winters are mild, with occasional rain, especially in the mountains, and snow at higher altitudes. Spring and autumn are the best times for touring the inland areas.

Clothing

Take lightweight clothing in summer (cotton is most comfortable), with an extra layer for cool evenings. A raincoat, or at least an umbrella, will be useful in winter and spring.

Spanish people like to dress stylishly. Although they have come to tolerate tourist habits, beach wear is not appreciated in towns and cities, and certainly not in churches. A few more formal restaurants ask men to wear a jacket and tie.

Communications

The telephone system is modern and works well. To make an international call to Spain, dial the international access code followed by 34 and the local area code (minus the initial 9) and number.

To make an international call from Spain, dial 07, wait for a steady tone, then dial the country code (1 for Canada and the US, 44 for UK), area code (omitting initial 0 from UK numbers) and number. There are plenty of coin- and card-operated phones. Cards for 1000 or 2000 pesetas can be bought from post offices and *estancos* (tobacconists' shops). You can also call from Telefónica offices and private telephone shops, paying at the end of the call.

Cellular phones operating on European-standard GSM will work in Spain.

It generally costs much more to use the phone in your hotel room, unless you use one of the calling cards issued by international telephone companies. Fax messages can be sent and received through many hotels.

Postal services work, although quite slowly. Airmail reaches most European destinations in 4 to 6 days. Shops that sell postcards rarely if ever have stamps; for those you will have to go to a post office or an *estanco* (tobacconists).

Crime

Street crime in the cities is a problem so take normal precautions: avoid dark or lonely places at night, beware of pickpockets in crowded places; don't carry large amounts of cash or wear valuable jewellery.

Don't leave anything on show when parking your car. Use guarded car parks if you can, remove the car radio and leave the glove box open—and empty. Leave *nothing* in a car overnight.

Driving

Major roads are generally good and well-surfaced; minor country and mountain roads may be poor. Sometimes you will see a big sign saying PELIGRO; it means "Danger".

Drive on the right and always park pointing in the same direction as the traffic. Seat belts must be worn, and the law requires cars to carry a red triangle to display in case of breakdown in the roadway, and a spare set of bulbs for the lights.

Speed limits for cars are 50 km/hr (31 mph) in built-up areas, 90–100 km/hr (56–62 mph) outside towns, 120 km/hr (75 mph) on *autovías* or *autopistas* (motorways) and otherwise as marked. There are a few sections of toll motorway in southern Spain, and because the charges are rather high these are underused.

Driving in cities can be frustrating, with frequent delays and few parking places. When visiting, find a safe, preferably guarded, parking place and walk or take taxis.

Be prepared for other drivers to do surprising things, stopping or turning suddenly without warning. If you have an accident, try to inform the police, or ensure that someone else does. If anyone is injured, you may be detained until blame is allocated. If you take your own vehicle to Spain, you will need to make certain that you are fully insured, and to obtain a "bail bond". (Check with your insurance company or motoring organization.)

Emergencies

To call the National Police dial 091, or Guardia Civil on 062; the Fire Service 080 (in some places 085); Medical Emergencies 061.

For an Ambulance numbers vary—2303034 applies to most of the Costa del Sol. Do not expect the respondent to understand English. European emergency number is 112.

Essentials

Sun screen cream (a high protection factor is essential except in winter), a sun hat, dark glasses, film and any medicines you may need—the same brands may not be available.

Etiquette

Always greet someone before saying anything else or asking a question. It is usual to shake hands when meeting people, and when taking leave of them.

Formalities

Citizens of European Union countries can enter with a national identity card or passport. Visas are not needed by travellers from western European countries, Canada and New Zealand, but Australian citizens do need a visa. US citizens may stay for up to 90 days without a visa.

Local and foreign currency may be imported, although amounts above 500,000 pesetas should be declared. You may take the following into Spain duty-free: 200 cigarettes or 50 cigars or 250 g tobacco; 1 litre of spirits (liquor) and 1 bottle of wine; a reasonable quantity of perfume and eau de toilette. Entering from other EU countries, larger quantities of tax- and duty-paid goods may be carried (800 cigarettes, 90 litres of wine and 110 litres of beer, for personal use).

Health and Medical Matters

After a long flight, relax for a couple of days. Doctors suggest eating lightly, and avoiding too much sun. In hot weather, drink plenty of water, wear a sunhat, use a sunscreen with a high protection factor (at least 20) and make sure that children do the same.

The tap water is safe in cities and towns. Pharmacies sell a wide variety of medications, but some will be under unfamiliar names.

It is advisable to take out comprehensive travel insurance, including coverage of medical expenses. EU nationals can get free emergency treatment—it helps if they carry a qualifying document (for UK citizens the Form E111) obtainable from post offices before leaving home. Keep receipts for any payments you have to make, in order to claim refunds.

Language

Spanish is the national language. The Andalusian dialect differs somewhat from the Castilian spoken in Madrid, mainly in that the endings of words are often shortened or disappear altogether, and the soft 'c' (in 'ci' and 'ce') and 'z' are not lisped, sounding like 's', not 'th'. And 'll' sounds like 'y', not like the 'll' in million.

English is widely understood, but if you try to learn and use a few polite phrases in Spanish your efforts will be greatly appreciated.

Media

State-run and commercial TV channels are augmented in many hotels by satellite and cable channels, including BBC World, Sky, CNN, German, French and Italian channels. Some radio stations on the Costa del Sol have English news and other programmes, and Gibraltar stations can also be picked up.

Newspapers in English are widely available. Some UK papers print editions in Spain, available in the morning. Otherwise, UK papers arrive in most places by early evening on the day of publication.

Money

The currency is the *peseta* (pta), with banknotes from 1,000 to 10,000 and coins from 1 to 500 ptas.

Foreign currency and traveller's cheques may be changed at banks, exchange offices and 61 large hotels (at a less favourable rate). Major credit cards are very widely accepted. Using them or bank cards, cash may be obtained from ATMs (automatic teller machines) outside banks, if you know the PIN (personal identification number).

Opening Hours

Museums and other attractions generally open from 9.30 or 10 a.m. to about 5.30 p.m. (later in summer). Some close on Monday, and many close from 1.30 to 4 p.m. It is worth checking in advance.

Shops usually open from 9.30 or 10 a.m. to 1 p.m., and again from 4.30 or 5 p.m. to 7.30 p.m. or later, Monday to Saturday.

Post offices open from 8.30 a.m. to 2.30 p.m., Monday to Friday, 9.30 a.m. to 1 p.m. Saturday.

Banks open from 9 a.m. to 2 p.m., Monday to Friday, 9 a.m. to 1 p.m. Saturday, except in summer. Exchange offices keep longer hours.

Photography and Video

Colour print film is widely available in the cities; transparency film is harder to find. Colour prints can be processed locally, within an hour in some places, but quality cannot be guaranteed. Transparency film is best taken back to your own country for processing.

Video-tape is available. Pre-recorded tapes are compatible with most of Europe, but not the US.

Public Holidays

January 1	New Year's Day
January 6	Epiphany
February 28	Andalusia Regional Holiday
May 1	Labour Day
August 15	Assumption
October 12	Hispanity Day
November 1	All Saints'
December 6	Constitution Day
December 8	Immaculate Conception
December 25	Christmas

Moveable holidays:
Maundy Thursday (March–April)
Good Friday (March–April)

Public Transport

Bus companies run regular services between all the main cities and towns, starting from central bus stations or the company's own terminal. Within cities, taxis are readily available. If they don't have meters, agree the fare in advance.

Trains can be a good way to travel between the cities. Málaga, Córdoba, Granada, Seville, Jerez, Cádiz and Ronda are all served by RENFE, the state-run railway. The Talgo express connects Madrid and Málaga, and the high-speed AVE between Madrid and

Seville (via Córdoba) takes only about three hours.

Religion

The majority of people are Catholic, although church attendance is in decline amongst the younger generation and some church teaching—such as that on birth control—is widely ignored.

For the large foreign population, resident and transient, of the Costa del Sol, there are various Protestant churches, synagogues and mosques.

Tax Refunds

If you live outside the European Union, you can recover the sales tax, known as IVA in Spain, on large purchases. Shops will tell you the limits, and will provide the necessary documents. These must be shown to customs, with the goods, on departure.

Everyone benefits from tax-free and duty-free shopping in Gibraltar, but strict limits apply when you re-enter Spain.

Time

Spain is on GMT + 1, advancing to GMT + 2 between April and October. It is one hour ahead of the UK and Ireland.

Tipping

Restaurant bills include a service charge, but waiters have come to expect a tip as well. In informal bars and cafés, it's the custom to leave some small change. Taxi-drivers expect fares to be rounded up by about 10%, and a small tip is usually given to porters and cloakroom attendants.

Toilets

Variously labelled *aseos*, *servicios* or *WC*, clean public lavatories are provided at most tourist attractions. Bars and cafés have them—it is polite to buy a drink or coffee.

Tourist Information

Airports and all resorts and major towns have a Tourist Office (*Oficina de Turismo*), open from 9 or 10 a.m. to 1 or 2 p.m., and sometimes from 4 p.m. to 7 p.m., Monday to Saturday. Most of them have excellent information leaflets and maps of the local area; there may be a small charge for these.

Voltage

The electrical supply is 220V, 50 Hz, AC. Plugs are of the mainland European type, with two round pins. Any 110V equipment needs a transformer as well as an adapter.

Water

Tap water is safe to drink in the main towns and cities, although many people prefer bottled water —check that the seal is unbroken.

INDEX

General editor: Barbara Ender-Jones
Editor: Mark Little
Design: Luc Malherbe
Photos: Ken Welsh
Maps: Elsner & Schichor, JPM Publications

Copyright © 1998 by JPM Publications S.A.
12, avenue William-Fraisse, 1006 Lausanne, Switzerland
E-mail: information@jpmguides.com
Web site: http://www.jpmguides.com/

Gibraltar

Pillar of Hercules

An awesome portal to the Mediterranean, the Rock of Gibraltar rises 426 m (1,396 ft) out of the sea. Known to the ancient world as one of the Pillars of Hercules and long famous for its hospitality to visiting ships, the Rock has been under British sovereignty since 1704.

Although linked to the Spanish mainland, Gibraltar has a distinctive character, in some ways like Britain a generation ago. Its people—variously of Italian, Iberian, Maltese, Jewish Moroccan and Indian descent—are united in their insistence on preserving the British connection.

To Spain, the anomaly is a constant irritant. In 1969, when Britain failed to comply with a United Nations resolution that called for "decolonization", Spain closed the border for 16 years. Telephone links were cut, the ferry to Algeciras was stopped and Spanish workers could no longer take jobs in Gibraltar. But the UN also said that the views of the 30,000 Gibraltarians should be taken into consideration, and a referendum produced a 99 per cent vote to stay British.

As a condition of Spanish entry to the European Union, the border was re-opened in 1985. Now, day trippers from Spain come in their thousands for sightseeing and bargain shopping; the people and the blue-helmeted British-style "bobbies" chat to them in English or Spanish with equal ease.

Spain has proposed a period of joint sovereignty, to be followed by reversion to Spain, but most Gibraltarians reject the idea. The British government is committed to respecting their wishes, although the strategic importance of the Rock has practically vanished, and most British forces have left. New sources of jobs and prosperity are needed: financial services already take advantage of Gibraltar's status as a tax haven, modern offices and apartment buildings are springing up, and new land has been created by filling in part of the harbour. The town has been spruced up, tourism is being promoted and a new cruise ship terminal opened in 1997.

Hot dry summer days are freshened by a breeze blowing through the Straits. When the eastern wind blows, a misty cloud, the Levanter, hangs over the Rock. Winters are mild with occasional rain. Many visitors combine a few days on the Rock with a holiday in Spain or Morocco. Gibraltar's airport is convenient for nearby Spanish golf courses and resorts; regular flights serve several Moroccan destinations and frequent ferries sail to Tangier.

A Brief History

Prehistory	Gibraltar's caves are home to some of the last Neanderthal people. They die out around 27,000 BC, and the ancestors of modern humans move in.
Early history	In about 800 BC, Phoenicians from the eastern Mediterranean found the city of Carteia on the nearby mainland; their ships trade as far away as Britain. The Carthaginians later inherit southern Spain including the Rock, but lose it to the Romans in about 200 BC. With the decline of Roman power, it falls to the Vandals in the 5th century AD and then to the Visigoths. Carteia becomes one of the first Christian communities in Spain.
8th–14th centuries	An Arab-led Muslim army under Tarik ibn-Ziyad crosses from North Africa, lands near Gibraltar in 711 and quickly conquers most of Spain. In his honour, the Rock is called Jebel al-Tarik (from which the name Gibraltar is derived).
15th–17th centuries	The Spanish kingdom of Castile recaptures the Rock on 29 August 1462. It becomes an important fortress and naval base.
18th–19th centuries	The Habsburg King Carlos II of Spain dies in 1700, leaving no heir. Disputes over who should take the throne lead to the War of the Spanish Succession (1702–13). Britain and the Netherlands support the Austrian Habsburg claimant. On 21 July, 1704, after three days of bombardment, 2,300 British and Dutch troops storm ashore and take Gibraltar. The Treaty of Utrecht which ends the war awards Britain sovereignty over the Rock. From 1779 to 1783 it withstands attack by French and Spanish forces in the Great Siege, and serves as a vital base for the British navy in the Napoleonic Wars.
20th century	Gibraltar plays a major role in the two world wars, keeping the route into the Mediterranean open to British and Allied ships. Early in World War II, almost the entire civilian population is evacuated to Britain, Madeira and Jamaica, returning between 1944 and 1951. Spain presses for British withdrawal and in 1969, the UN assembly passes a resolution favouring the Spanish case. Spain imposes border restrictions. These are lifted in 1985 but the issue of sovereignty remains in dispute. Meanwhile, Gibraltar has gained a wide measure of self-government. 67

Sightseeing

Gibraltar is only just over 5 km (3 miles) long and no more than 1.6 km (1 mile) across, but it is packed with interest.

On the Spanish side of the border, the town of La Línea has grown rapidly in recent times—many of its people work in Gibraltar. Frontier formalities are simple, but there may be a line of traffic, especially at morning rush hour. Just beyond the border is the airport terminal, from where you can walk or take a bus or taxi across the expanse of the airport runway to the town. Ahead is the near-vertical north face of the Rock; the holes visible halfway up are 18th-century cannon ports.

Gibraltar's **walls** were built by the Moors and reinforced by the Spanish and British. Here on the north side are two ramparts, with a produce **market** in between. Through the main gate in the old town, parallel streets run north-south and narrow lanes climb eastward from the harbour, ever more steeply as they rise up the slopes. At first sight the centre looks like an English Victorian town, but behind this layer are Spanish buildings from the 15th to 17th centuries. And beneath it all are the foundations of the old Moorish town.

Main Street, partly pedestrianized, is lined with shops offering electronic equipment, duty-free cameras, drinks, perfume and cigarettes. Interspersed with these are pubs, banks and branches of chain stores, familiar to visitors from the UK.

To the right down Bomb House Lane, **Gibraltar Museum** is housed in two old mansions. Exhibits tell the Gibraltar story from prehistoric to modern times; a large scale model picks out the main sites including caves and tunnels, and a video show relates the Rock's history. Excavations in the museum's own cellars have revealed spacious 14th century **Moorish Baths**, with hot, tepid, steam and cold rooms and a plunge bath. **Tourist information** is available in the Museum and in the Tourism Office, Cathedral Square.

Further along Main Street, **The Convent** has been the residence of the governor since 1728—it was a previously a convent of Franciscan friars. The soldiers on duty at its door carry out a frequent **Changing of the Guard** ceremony.

Referendum Gates in the southern walls commemorate the vote to stay British. Just beyond them is **Trafalgar Cemetery**, with graves of some who died of wounds here following the 1805 battle. (Those who were killed had been buried at sea except for Nelson: his body was preserved in brandy and taken to England.)

GIBRALTAR

Gibraltar Airport

Eastern Beach

Moorish Castle

Upper Galleries

Queensway

Main Street

Gibraltar Harbour

Old Queen's Road

Signal Station Road

Catalan Bay Village

Catalan Bay

Cable Car

Apes Den

Alameda Gardens

Sandy Bay

St. Michael's Cave

Engineer Road

Europa Road

Rosia Bay

Governor's Beach

BAY OF GIBRALTAR

Camp Bay

Little Bay

N

MEDITERRANEAN SEA

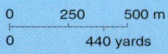

0   250   500 m

0   440 yards

Europa Point

Next comes the open space of **Grand Parade** and the green, tree-shaded **Alameda Botanical Gardens**, established in the 19th century.

Most of the **Upper Rock** has been designated a nature reserve. It is home to many unusual plants, and migratory birds use it as a stepping stone, southbound in autumn, northbound in spring. One ticket (or the cable car fare) covers entry to all the sights. Minibus-taxis offer a **Rock Tour**, including as many optional stops as you have time for, but the quickest way to reach the top is by the **cable car** from Grand Parade. There's an intermediate station near **Apes' Den**, one of several places where the Rock's resident Barbary apes congregate—because food is put out for them. They are in fact not apes, but tail-less macaque monkeys which were probably introduced by British sailors and escaped to live in a semi-wild state. Tradition says that if they die out, British sovereignty will end. (In World War II, Winston Churchill ordered that they be well fed!)

The terrace of the café at the **Upper Station** commands a superb view; west over the harbour; north to the airport and Spain; east down the steep slopes of old water catchments to Sandy Bay; and south to Europa Point and its lighthouse, and all the way

across the Straits of Gibraltar to the mountains of Morocco.

To the south along a path is **O'Hara's Battery**, the Rock's highest point, with a century-old 9.2-inch gun still pointing out to sea. A road south from Upper Station leads to **St Michael's Cave**, part of a system of limestone caverns which honeycomb the Rock. One chamber is set up as a theatre where occasional concerts are held amid the stalactites and stalagmites: during World War II it was made ready to use as a hospital.

Instead of descending by cable car, you can walk down to the southern end of the Rock, or take a longer stroll north to the **Upper Galleries** (reached by an uphill track near Princess Caroline's

70

Battery). Entrance is by the Great Siege Tunnel, excavated using gunpowder between 1779–83, with openings in the rock face for cannon. A World War II extension cuts through to a lookout point on the east side of the Rock. In all, 53 km (33 miles) of tunnels have been dug within the Rock; here, several hundred metres are open, with good historical displays. Downhill from the tunnel entrance is the outdoor **Gibraltar Under Siege** exhibition, describing life in the 18th century for the garrison and people at war.

Further down (or reached by a short, steep walk from the northern end of the town) is the **Moorish Castle**, battered in a dozen sieges. In its 14th-century Tower of Homage a room is set up as a mosque.

The eastern side of the Rock drops steeply to the sea, with the village of **Catalan Bay** facing one of four small sandy beaches enjoying the morning sun. Two more beaches on the southwest corner are popular with windsurfers, and tour boats make sightseeing, fishing and dolphin-spotting trips in the bay.

Eating Out

Traditional British dishes are on the menu in many restaurants and pubs, including fish and chips, shepherd's pie, roast beef and Yorkshire pudding and an "all-day breakfast" of eggs and bacon, sausage and tomato. English-style tearooms serve afternoon tea with cakes and pastries.

For variety, Gibraltar can offer Italian, Indian, Chinese, Moroccan and kosher restaurants. Following the Spanish model, a few bars feature *tapas*, small, reasonably priced portions of appetizers served with drinks. They might include seafood such as *calamares* (squid) or *pulpo* (octopus), salads, olives or potato and onion omelette.

The range of drinks is vast: British, Spanish and various other beers, the wines and spirits (liquors) of the world and every sort of soft drink.

Shopping

Duty-free status and no VAT mean rock-bottom prices for drinks and cigarettes. Petrol is also quite a lot cheaper than in Spain, so when the wait at the border is short, Spanish drivers cross over just to fill up.

For other items such as cameras, video-cameras and electronic equipment, savings are not enormous. It is worth comparing prices and trying a little bargaining—at least by asking for discounts on any pretext. Check if possible that you are getting the latest model, and that electrical goods are compatible with your home supply.

Practical Information

Banks. Open 9 a.m. to 3.30 p.m., Monday to Friday; some open until 6 p.m. on Friday afternoon.

Credit cards and traveller's cheques are widely accepted.

Currency. The unit of currency is the *pound sterling* (£), divided into 100 pence (p). Gibraltar and UK banknotes and coins are both in use, banknotes in denominations from £5 to £50, and coins from 1p to £1. Spanish pesetas are also accepted in most shops.

Electric current. 230 volts AC, 50Hz. Plugs have three flat pins, as in UK.

Emergencies. For police or ambulance services, dial 199, for fire brigade 190. Calls are free.

Post offices. Open 9 a.m. to 5.30 p.m. Monday to Friday and 9 a.m. to 12.30 p.m. on Saturdays.

Shops. Open 10 a.m. to 7 p.m. Monday to Friday, 10 a.m. to 1 p.m. Saturday.

Telephones. Coin- and card-operated telephones are widely available. To phone abroad (except Spain), dial 00 (international access code), the country code, area code and number. For calls to Spain, dial the area code and number only. Dialling code to call Gibraltar is 350 or, from Spain, 9567.

Time. Gibraltar keeps European Continental time, the same as Spain: GMT + 2 from April through October, GMT + 1 the rest of the year.

Tipping. A service charge is included in bills at hotels and some restaurants; at others a tip of 10 per cent or more is added for good service. Porters and hairdressers are tipped. Taxi drivers expect a tip of about 10 per cent of the fare.

Water. Tap water is drinkable.

Photo: MARKA, Milano

Tangier

Worldly Crossroads

Tangier is so near to Spain that you can almost hear the wail of a flamenco singer wafting across the Strait of Gibraltar. As the gateway to North Africa, lying at the crossroads of the Mediterranean and the Atlantic, the city is bound to be cosmopolitan; so many nationalities have settled here, ruled here, or flamboyantly passed through, that Tangier has always been a focus for international intrigue and the home of eccentric characters. It now tends to revel in its former notoriety rather than sprucing itself up.

Although tolerance reigns, you needn't expect to find a Hollywood cast of smugglers, spies and gangsters. The local people, who cheerfully call themselves Tangerines, have seen it all. But now it is more the conventional tourist who is attracted by the sunshine and atmosphere of *laissez-faire*.

Tangier's chequered history goes back at least 3,000 years. The Phoenicians, whose commercial empire stretched from present-day Lebanon to the Strait of Gibraltar and beyond, set up a trading post and fishing port. They were followed by Carthaginians and, later, the Romans, who occupied the town they called Tingis for five centuries. The Arabs arrived in the 8th century and used Tangier as a base for their conquest of Spain. In the 15th century Tangier was captured by Portugal, and for a time it belonged to England. But the most extraordinary episode was yet to come: in 1906 the city was put under the control of a consortium of eight European powers. With Moroccan independence in 1956, Tangier was reunited with the rest of the nation.

And today the city (population around 500,000) is as Moroccan as couscous, calligraphy or snake charmers. You need only enter the medina, the old town of narrow streets and blind alleys, to be immersed in this timeless society of craftsmen, merchants and veiled women. If you get lost, there's an absolute embarrassment of volunteer guides who know a few words of many languages beyond their native Arabic. The most widely-spoken second language is Spanish, for this part of the country used to be governed by Spain.

After you've explored the souk and the casbah and seen the view over the harbour and across the strait to Spain, stroll through the modern quarter with its boulevards, parks, shops and cafés. Stop for a fragrant mint tea, and munch a pastry as delicate as it is sweet. You don't have to be a smuggler, a spy or a gangster to appreciate the simple pleasures of Tangier.

A Brief History

12th century BC	The Phoenicians found a trading post and fishing base at Tangier. The Carthaginians follow but are soon vanquished by the Romans.
1st century BC	The Romans rule Tangier from administrative head-quarters in Spain. Under the name Tingis, the town serves as the capital of the Roman province of Tingitan Mauritania.
5th–11th centuries AD	In the 5th century the Vandals take Tangier; Dark Ages follow. The Arabs conquer Tangier and use it as a staging post for their invasion of Spain in 711. The Almoravids, founders of Morocco's golden age, capture the town in 1075.
15th–17th centuries	The Portuguese seize Tangier in 1471 and transform the main mosque into a cathedral. In 1661 Tangier is presented to Charles II of England as part of Catherine of Braganza's dowry. Sultan Moulay Ismail captures Tangier from besieged English forces in 1684.
19th–20th centuries	Tangier becomes a commercial base and has a large European colony. In 1923 it becomes a tax-free International Zone. When Morocco gains independence in 1956, Tangier is incorporated into the kingdom.

Sightseeing

Two traditional centres of Tangier life are called the Grand Socco and the Petit Socco, the big and small markets. In Tangerine style, the names mix French, Spanish and Arabic words without awkwardness or untoward affectation.

The **Grand Socco**, the big souk, occupies a large square officially called the Place du 9 Avril 1947, just outside the old town walls. From here you walk through an archway into the medina, a bustling hillside of winding streets and lanes, an area divided into mini-neighbourhoods in which artisans of different trades congregate—there is the street of the woodworkers, another for jewellers. You'll be able to sniff out a whole range of aromas—pungent spices, the heady perfume of flowers and the mouth-watering smell of kebabs grilling over charcoal.

The **Petit Socco**, in the heart of the medina, is a pleasant open space with several cafés. All 75

Tangier passes by here—businessmen in striped jellabas, women in caftans or Paris dresses, and a mischievous cast of children.

At the top of the hill above the medina, the **Casbah** (citadel) seems impregnable from land or sea. This fortress was the centre of administration of old Tangier, where the great Alaouite Sultan Moulay Ismail chose to build his palace behind the batteries of cannon installed on the walls after he captured the city from the British in 1684..

Along Rue Riad Sultan, a large unmarked doorway opens onto a pretty courtyard, revealing ivy- and vine-covered trellises, orange trees and twittering birds. This is the **Sultan's Garden**, part of Moulay Ismail's 17th-century palace, **Dar el Makhzen**. To enter the palace, you have to cross another small garden, dominated by a giant triple-trunk fig tree. The beautiful interior court, surrounded by rotund marble columns, is the centre of the palace's **Museum of Moroccan Arts**. The exhibition rooms cover all manner of arts and crafts, from priceless illuminated Korans to wood and metal work, as well as Berber carpets, fine textiles and a collection of ceramics. The adjoining **Antiquities Museum** goes as far back as Stone Age finds and Roman mosaics.

You can leave the palace by the elegant treasury, **Bit el Mal**, where several rooms with a balcony overlook the *méchouar*, the paradeground on which the crowds assembled to pay tribute to the sultan or governor. North of the *méchouar*, an observation point atop the cliff offers Tangier's best view of the harbour and the strait.

Near the southeast corner of the medina is the **Great Mosque**, another contribution of Sultan Moulay Ismail. It was built over the ruins of an old mosque which the Portuguese had converted into the Cathedral of the Holy Spirit in the 15th century.

Leading south from the Grand Socco, the Rue de la Liberté goes to the very centre of the modern city of Tangier—the Place de France and Boulevard Pasteur. Cafés, restaurants, travel agencies and bookstores are all within a few streets, and there's a fine panorama of the harbour and the Spanish mainland from the **terrace** along the boulevard—a good place, too, to watch the life of the city from the vantage point of a café table.

Excursions

On a hot summer day it's a relief to head for **La Montagne** (The Mountain)—a hilly area west of the city where the rich businessmen and expatriates have their

© 1995 by JPM Publications SA

Belvédère

Jardins
du Sultan

KASBAH

Dar el
Makhzen

Bab Haha

Bab el Assa

Rue de la Kasbah

Bab el
Bahar

Rue Ibn Al Abbar

MÉDIA

Grande
Mosquée

PORT

Mosquée

Petit
Socco

Avenue Hassan I

Rue d'Italie

Jardins Mendoubia

Rue Es Siaghin

Poste

Bab Fahs

Rue Bourrakia

Mosquée

Grand
Socco

Marché

Rue du Portugal

Sidi Bouabib

Eglise
St-André

Cimetière
juif

Gare

Rue d'Angleterre

Rue de la Liberté

Rue de la Plage

Avenue d'Espagne

Rue Hollande

Théâtre

Rue de Belgique

Place
Mohammed V

Boulevard Pasteur

Office du
Tourisme

Sacré
Cœur

Rue du Mexique

Rue de Fès

Rue Moussa Noussaïr

Boulevard Mohammed V

Poste

Rue Jeanne d'Arc

Rue du Prince Héritier

TANGIER

0   250   500 m
0   275   550 yd

villas. There is a palace here, too, so that the royal family can escape the heat of the imperial cities to the south. The coast beyond The Mountain is tempered by refreshing breezes.

At Cap Spartel, a **lighthouse** more than a century old stares out at all the supertankers sailing between the Atlantic and the Mediterranean. You can climb the spiral staircase to the observation level for a better look.

Robinson Beach is an inviting, endless expanse of sand but the tides make it extremely risky for swimming. A few miles down the coast you can wander among the **Caves of Hercules**, where prehistoric people quarried stone. The fortified town and fishing port of **Asilah** is 40 km (25 miles) further down the coast.

An all-day excursion into the Rif Mountains features the delightful town of Chaouen, otherwise known as Chécha-ouen or Xauen, 120 km (75 miles) southeast of Tangier. There's a stop on the way at the modern city of **Tetouan**, once notorious as a nest of pirates and more recently the capital of the Spanish protectorate of northern Morocco. The city traces its history back more than 2,000 years, but the modern phase began at the end of the 15th century when Muslim and Jewish refugees from the Christian Reconquest of Spain flooded in.

They brought with them the skills of Andalusian architects, artists and artisans. The medina, with wrought-iron balconies and colourful tile decorations, is the ultimate Mauresque medina in Morocco.

From its dramatic setting between rocky mountain peaks and precipitous defiles, **Chaouen** surveys the hills around and the valleys below. The architecture tells the history of this surprising town: a typical Moroccan medina co-exists with a classic Spanish town plaza complete with topiary arches, grape arbours and tiled benches around a central fountain.

Founded in the 15th century, Chaouen was isolated from the rest of the country for hundreds of years, and the inhabitants maintained their Andalusian architecture, gardens and handicrafts. The modern Spanish era ended in 1956 with Moroccan independence. Though the red tile roofs and other Spanish touches remain, it's clear that Islam rules today in Chaouen. Up from Plaza el Makhzen, with its painted arcades and small shops, is a centuries-old casbah, recently restored. Its gardens, planted with palm trees and flowers, are a haven of tranquillity. In the souks and bazaars of the medina you can bargain over the output of the local carpet factories.

Eating Out

Moroccan cuisine features plenty of hearty country cooking plus some sublime surprises. One of these last is *bstilla* or pigeon pie. The birds are stuffed and cooked, and then the meat is spread in layers of flaky pastry along with saffron, almonds, sugar and cinnamon, and baked to a perfect and triumphant crispness.

Couscous can be found everywhere: tiny steamed grains of semolina topped with stewed vegetables and meat, accompanied by hot and spicy *harissa*.

Tajine is an all-purpose stew, named after the earthenware pot in which it is traditionally prepared. It might contain tomatoes, peas, beans, carrots, aubergines (eggplant), marrow (squash), and chunks of lamb, veal or beef.

You can enjoy charcoal-grilled kebabs (skewers of lamb, beef, liver or heart) in restaurants and at roadside stands.

Fresh fish and seafood abound. Mullet, dorado or sea perch may be grilled or poached, or marinated and then baked or stewed.

Even small and modest restaurants stock a few good local wines, such as *cabernet* (red and rosé), *valpierre* (red and white), *vieux pape* (red) and *oustalet* (rosé and white). The French legacy also appears in the large assortment of apéritif wines found in Tangier bars and cafés.

Shopping

Morocco leather, fine-grained and soft, is used to cover books and desk utensils. Goods made of sturdier leather are also popular: pouffes, suitcases, handbags, camel saddles and *babouches* (slippers).

To recreate the Arabian nights atmosphere at home, you can buy a caftan or jellaba, local fashions for women and men.

In many shops and stalls you'll be offered large copper or brass trays with elaborate hammered designs; together with a small folding stand these make useful and attractive little tables. Pottery is another good buy.

Moroccan carpets generally have a looser weave and a deeper pile than the more intricate Persian or Turkish carpets.

Antique muskets and daggers are often on sale, though their "antiquity" is open to question. In any case, such weapons were still in use in Morocco well into the 20th century.

Some of the smarter shops have fixed prices and will tell you so, but elsewhere the chances are good that the merchant is willing to bargain. Visit a few shops to compare prices before you begin serious haggling. Energetic negotiators may end up paying less than half the initially quoted price. But keep smiling and don't lose your temper.

Practical Information

Photos: Jean-Claude Vieillefond

Credit cards and traveller's cheques. The large hotels and best restaurants usually accept credit cards. Be sure to have your passport with you when you use credit cards or traveller's cheques. And keep the exchange slips; you'll need them if you want to change your left-over dirhams as you leave Morocco.

Currency. The Moroccan *dirham*, abbreviated *DH*, is divided into 100 *centimes*. You'll rarely see coins of less than 1 dirham. Banknotes come in denominations from 10 to 200 dirhams. Moroccan merchants will often use the word *francs* when they mean centimes.

Language. Arabic is the official language, with Spanish the second language in Tangier and French the third.

Opening hours. Banks open Monday to Friday from 8.15 to 11.30 a.m. and again from 2.15 to 4 p.m. However, in summer they operate non-stop from 8 a.m. to 3 p.m. And during Ramadan the schedule is 9.30 a.m. to 2 p.m. Shops in the medinas tend to operate from 8 a.m. to 9 p.m. daily, with a break for prayers on Friday.

Telephone. To make an international call dial 00 then the country code (1 for the US and Canada, 44 for the UK), the area code minus the initial zero and the local number.

Tipping. Restaurant: service charge included, a tip for the waiter of 5–10 per cent is optional. Lavatory attendant: 1 dirham. Porter: 1–2 dirhams per bag. Taxi driver: round up the fare.

Water. Tap water is normally safe, but bottled mineral waters are always available in restaurants, cafés and hotels.